Raising Badass Kids

The Savvy Parents' Guide to Predator-Proofing Tweens & Teens

By CJ Scarlet

Table of Contents

Dedication

This book is dedicated to Carter, Abby, and Elliott for inspiring me to share my wisdom to keep you safe and to protect other kids in the process. I love you more than life itself!

To my dear friend John Mitterling, whose kindness, generosity, and integrity are an inspiration.

I'd also like to dedicate this book to you–the badass reading these words—for parenting up and doing your best to ensure your precious child's safety.

&

At the end of this book, you'll find information about my 21-Day Action Plan that will help you implement the advice I share here, so you raise a badass kid who knows how to avoid dangerous people and to protect and defend themselves.

Following this easy and clear action plan will allow you to establish a closer relationship with your child, leading to engaging, two-way conversations that show them you're paying attention and have their back.

It will also enable you to spot problems, clear up misunderstandings, and open up opportunities to talk at a deeper level about any issues that are on your kid's mind—*making YOU a seriously badass parent!*

Foreword

Raise your hand if you were taught "don't talk to strangers" as you were growing up. This old advice, as unhelpful and inaccurate as it is, was the main message I received as a kid. My parents meant well, but they had not been taught anything about child safety, so despite their best efforts, they had little to teach me. Before the 1980s, "Predator Proofing" was barely even a concept!

The good news is that generation by generation, we have *learned a lot more* about how to prevent abuse and recognize dangerous situations early so they can be stopped at the earliest possible moment. CJ Scarlet's powerful voice speaks across generations. Her Badass Grandma wisdom can wake you up, shake you by the shoulders, and give you solid guidance about what to look out for and how to respond to protect the kids in your life.

As a child safety expert, my approach is a little different than CJ's. Her Badass Grandma voice and approach are uniquely her own. You'll see–she is an original who just can't be copied! The fact remains, though, that at the foundational level, we are operating on a common set of core principles. I think it's cool to see that.

CJ's voice is no-nonsense, blunt, and she gets right to the heart of the matter. She has a wealth of experience and information to share. And she does it in a way that resonates with today's parents.

Child safety is an all-hands-on-deck effort. CJ and I both believe deeply that child safety starts at home and extends into the world. Parents and other caring adults are the eyes, ears, and early warning and response systems on the lookout for safety problems. This is true within families, neighborhoods, schools, and organizations.

It helps to have allies, so bring your friends and colleagues along with you on this journey. This is an excellent opportunity for grassroots leadership to create positive change. Grassroots vigilance, and yes, even *pressure,* have been crucial in exposing serious cases of abuse and getting organizations to do the right thing to protect kids.

You can do this! Badass Grandma CJ Scarlet is here to show you how.

Amy Tiemann, PhD
Co-author of *Doing Right by Our Kids: Protecting
Child Safety at All Levels* and Kidpower International
Senior Program Leader

INTRODUCTION

Only the Smartiest of Pants Actually Read the Intro...

Wait. What? That headline doesn't make sense, but if you're a smarty pants, you get my drift.

And it's true! Did you know 90 percent of people don't read book introductions?[i] That's because they're not nearly as smart or progressive or—let's just say it—good-looking as you are.

Whether or not you believe yourself to be smart or attractive (you're the bee's knees, I promise!), please read this section; it sets the groundwork for the following chapters AND it's entertaining!

I want to begin by complimenting you on your incredible taste in books. *Raising Badass Kids* is the most comprehensive manual available to parents who want to teach their children ages 10 to 18 how to avoid danger and protect and defend themselves from sketchy people.

You—and your kid—have more power to protect them from predators than you may think. My biggest emphasis in this and my other books is on avoiding danger part because there's so much you both can do to keep them from ever becoming the target of bad people.

#MeToo is a great and necessary movement, but it focuses on "it happened to me." MY focus is on #NotMeToo and #NotMyKid—in other words, on preventing violence *before* it occurs.

---

i OK, I totally made up that statistic, but it's probably not too far from the truth.

The military refers to this as staying "left of bang." "Bang" is the actual assault; everything that precedes it, that you do to prevent it, is called "left of bang." What occurs after an encounter—what you do in response to the assault—is "right of bang."

You obviously want your child to stay left of bang by teaching them how to spot dangerous people and thwart an assault before it can take place. *Raising Badass Kids* will help you do exactly that.

This Isn't Your Momma's Parenting Book Because I Ain't Your Momma

Dr. Spock is rolling over in his grave, I'm sure, over the mere existence of this book.[ii] Put flatly, it's as irreverent as it gets. This gallows humor is my way of dealing with distressing topics so we don't get lost in the darkness.

I wrote the book to be snarky intentionally. It's mainly for GenXers and Millennials (and the generations that follow), and, well, it's hard as hell to get your attention. Your world today isn't even remotely close to the world I lived in when I was parenting in the '80s and '90s.

I'm not saying there weren't school shootings and bullies to deal with, but it wasn't, like, IN YOUR FACE EVERY SINGLE SECOND OF THE DAY, NO MATTER WHERE YOU LOOKED! AAAAAHHHHHH!

Yeah, the interwebs are great, but it also makes it appear that danger lurks around every corner, hovering over your kid, waiting to pounce. And social media? Ye Gods! It's a free-for-all!

Perfectly nice, "normal" people who wouldn't say boo to a goose in real life turn into complete monsters online, trolling people and spewing invective and even hate speech like it's nothing to be ashamed of.

Any one of us can be a target, but parents are a special favorite of SPPTs (Supposedly Perfect Parent Trolls) who catch a tiny snippet of others'

---

ii Dr. Benjamin Spock, not to be confused with Mr. Spock from Star Trek, was a pediatrician who wrote a mega bestselling book in 1946 entitled *The Common Sense Book of Baby and Child Care* that encouraged parents to pick up their kids once in a while. The book radically advised parents to see their kids as individuals, not just tiny slaves, and to be affectionate towards them.

"not-so-fine" parenting moments and lay them to utter waste, destroying reputations and self-esteem like Godzilla rampaging Tokyo.

These SPPTs post pictures of themselves laughing a little too hysterically while drinking (potentially spiked) hot cocoa with their SPKs (Supposedly Perfect Kids) and drive suspiciously clean minivans that look like they were cleaned by someone trying to cover up a crime scene. Every photo, video, opinion, or frustration shared by another parent online is taken out of context, dissected, distorted, and then harshly judged by a jury of their peers. Doesn't matter which side you're on; half the people not only disagree with it; they're going to insist that you're the devil incarnate and should be summarily shot.

These people take time from their busy-but-not-at-all-stressful lives to remind you how badly you're failing because your kid (gasp!) hasn't yet taken the PSAT, and your car looks like the crime scene *before* the serial killer broke out the Shop-Vac®.

Never have so many judged so many others so often based on so little evidence and aforethought. No wonder my daughter-in-law and every other young mom I've talked with feel like they can't possibly win this rigged parenting game.

Well, I'll tell you a little secret: It's all an elaborate hoax. There are no perfect moms or dads, and no one, not one single parent out there, knows with certainty what they're doing. We're all just winging it and praying we don't raise a serial killer of our own (although, on the plus side, his car would be very, very clean—just sayin').

Know that *I see you.* I see you doing your best under tremendous pressure and I think you're doing a kickass job. So, stop comparing your hot messy insides to other people's seemingly together outsides, and keep your attention where it belongs—on your kids.

Just like a Horror Movie, Only With a Happier Ending

While writing this guide, I struggled mightily with how to present the facts about childhood dangers without scaring you so badly you'd put the book down and never touch it again.

It's hard to discuss subjects as harrowing as sexual abuse, bullying, online dangers, and sex trafficking without dragging you and your child into a dark place that can lead to hopelessness and helplessness, which can morph into apathy and paralysis. Definitely, not a productive place to be when you're trying to protect your tween or teen.

I don't believe terrifying you will spur you to action, as most experts and authors on these topics appear to believe. After reading this book, I want you to feel confident in your newfound ability to talk candidly with your kid without scaring her to death.

Yes, I will lay out some of the facts and stats to let you know what you're up against, but in a way that's enlightening and not designed to sensationalize the information and scare the bejesus out of you.

Having said that, I *am* going to scare you initially because I want to juxtapose the petrifying facts you'll find on the internet and evening news with the more realistic data based on actual studies. So, let's begin.

The Awful, Horrible, Terrifying Facts

Did you know?

- Half of all children in the world experience some form of emotional, physical, or sexual abuse by the time they're 18.[1]
- Abusive experiences in childhood create fresh victims and predators, who often pass these experiences down from generation to generation.
- Survivors of child sexual abuse are 10 to 13 times more likely to attempt suicide.[2]
- Nearly 30 percent of active sex trafficking cases in the U.S. in 2022 involved children.[3]
- While kids today participate in regular active shooter drills at school, only the tiniest fraction get body safety training. When they do, the focus is often on "stranger danger" when, in fact, the vast majority of molestations and assaults are committed by people they know.[4]
- Eighty-nine percent of predators meet their victims online and through chat rooms.[5]

Quivering with fear yet? You're not alone. Most parents feel anxious when confronted with these jaw-dropping facts. They feel overwhelmed by the enormity of the problem and by their own lack of knowledge about how to prepare their kids to live in a world that's often hostile to them.

Parents are doing their best, but, to not scare their kids, they aren't being honest about the dangers they face. As such, *they're making their children more vulnerable to predators.* It's time to change this self-defeating, no-win situation and give your kid what he needs to live a safe, confident, happy life.

And Now for Something Completely Different

Okay, you can stop hyperventilating and take a deep breath. The world isn't as bad as the media makes it sound, and you and your kid have the power to keep him safe.

Let's balance the terrifying statistics listed above with a bit of perspective. When I used to hear that more than 400,000 children were missing and exploited each year, I envisioned kids being snatched off street corners by strangers every other minute. But that's NOT true!

Of the 359,094 children reported as missing or exploited in 2022:

- About 94 percent simply misunderstood directions or miscommunicated their plans, were lost, or ran away.[6]

- Five percent were kidnapped by family members involved in a custody dispute.[7]

- One percent were abducted by non-family members that the kids knew, usually during the commission of a crime, such as robbery or sexual assault.[8]

- Only around 105 children (less than 1 percent of all child victims[9]) are kidnapped each year in the stereotypical stranger abductions sensationalized on the evening news.[10] *(Of course, that's 105 too many!)* Of these, *just 65 predators were complete strangers.*[11]

- A whopping 99.8 percent of the children who go missing (whether abducted or runaways) return home.[12]

And a few more reassuring facts:

- The number of identified incidents of child sexual abuse has decreased by almost 50 percent since the 1990s.[13]
- Rates of sexual assault and domestic violence have been declining for decades and are now a quarter or less of their past peaks.[14]
- Since the early 1990s, the rate for all crimes—violent and nonviolent against both children and adults—has plummeted by up to 77 percent.[15]

We've Got It All Wrong

According to cognitive psychologist and author Steven Pinker, "Violence has been in decline for thousands of years, and today we may be living in the most peaceable era *in the existence of our species.*"[16] (Italics are mine.)

Despite these encouraging facts, nearly 90 percent of adults say they feel *less* safe than when they were growing up, even though today's crime rates are at a level not seen since the 1960s![17]

So, if crime rates in the U.S. and the world, in general, have gone down so dramatically, why do we remain convinced our kids are in grave peril if we let them out of our sight? I think it's because the teasers for the evening news assure us that if we don't watch their programs, we'll miss details of the latest ghastly shooting spree and *never* learn critical things like the three ways our toaster oven is plotting to murder our entire family while we sleep. It could also be that we binge-watch too many horrific crime dramas and shows filled with apocalyptic images of dead people who want to eat our brains.[iii]

We also worry because we're genetically hardwired to pay more attention to things that *appear* to pose an imminent threat than to stuff that seems unlikely to happen, say, being killed by a vending machine or a falling coconut (both of which happen more often than you'd think).

---

iii My biggest problem with being turned into a zombie would be all that walking! I'm frankly exhausted just thinking about it.

Parents are terrified of terrorist attacks and serial killers when in fact, their child is far more likely to be killed by a rogue champagne cork. Sure, it *could* happen, but are you really going to encase your kid in bubble wrap and make him waddle to school like a drunken leprechaun every day?

Bubble Wrap? Hmmm...

Clearly, you love and want to protect your kid from harm, or you wouldn't be reading this book. You may worry about his safety and want to arm him with information, but you don't want to leave him feeling petrified. You may have no idea what to say or how to say it, so he'll actually listen to and apply your cautionary advice.

Face it, you're not your child's BFF, and you shouldn't be. You're meant to be his protector, role model, gatekeeper, boundary teacher, motivator, sounding board, comforter, and, yes, accountability holder when needed.

You may want to wrap your child in a protective cocoon and defend him from every harm, but doing so could emotionally cripple him and make him MORE vulnerable to predators, not less. Teaching your kid to fear every stranger and new situation actually inhibits his intuitive wisdom that tells him when he's in danger.

Don't be afraid your sweetums will lose his innocence if you teach him about body safety. Won't happen. This is a cold, cruel world we live in, and your kid knows more than you realize. In fact, he'll be more empowered and far safer when he knows the dangers and how to meet them head-on. It's waaaay better to teach your child about sexual abuse, for example, than to pick up the pieces later because he didn't know how to protect himself.

A Word about Worry

I want to stop for a minute to talk about worry and how to release it because, frankly, it's freaking you and your kid out and making the situation worse. While it's important to be informed about the dangers your child faces, such knowledge is destructive when it spirals into worry and obsession over her safety.

Worrying is not a sustainable state; a normal person simply can't maintain that anxious state of mind and remain sane. Plus, it's shrinking your brain mass, making you age faster, and lowering your IQ. Look it up; it's science.

Author and personal protection expert Gavin De Becker notes that "Worry fights off that dreadful feeling that there's nothing we can do because worrying feels like we're doing something..." De Becker goes on, "When faced with some worry or uncertain fear, ask yourself: 'Am I responding to something in my environment or to something in my imagination?'" He advises that the best antidote to worry is *action*, which he addresses in his outstanding book *Protecting the Gift*.

Here's what I do when my mind starts wigging out at 3 a.m. as I envision something horrible happening to my grandbabies: As soon as I catch my thoughts spinning out of control, I close my eyes and say to myself, "*Control-Alt-Delete*" and then open my eyes. Those who aren't complete Luddites know that pressing "Control-Alt-Delete" on your keyboard will enable you to reboot your computer. Do this blinking exercise as often as it takes until the boogeyman in your head disappears.

You may think it sounds stupid or too simplistic, but I'm telling you there's something about mentally thinking "Control-Alt-Delete" and blinking your eyes that takes the needle off that murdery broken record playing in your head.

Stress expert Don Joseph Goewey notes, "Nature gave us a 90-second window to bust stressful thinking before it takes a long walk off a short pier."[18] Put plainly: The more you use techniques that divert stressful thoughts, the stronger the synapses that end worry become.

I love how Goewey explains this: "The part of the brain that causes stress reactions literally has the intelligence of a toddler. And every parent knows you don't stop a tantrum by appealing to a child's logic. You distract the child."

Techniques like my clever blink mantra distract your mind's terrible two-year-old and keep it from running amok. Next time you can't sleep because you have visions of predatory sugarplums dancing in your head, try using the "Control-Alt-Delete" maneuver and get some sleep!

Because I Said So! Or Why You Should Listen to Me

Who on earth am I to advise parents on keeping their kids safe? Well, I'm a danger expert, victim advocate for the past 33 years, and author of four books on personal safety. I'm also the survivor of childhood molestations and sexual assault as a college freshman, offering me the unenviable perspective of a crime victim.

I served as executive director of a child advocacy center for abused children and as Director of Victims' Issues for the NC Attorney General's Office. I hold an interdisciplinary master's degree in human violence. I volunteered for Safe Child's "Funny Tummy" program, which teaches first graders how to say no and tell if they encounter dangerous people. I also continue my work with survivors of child abuse, domestic violence, and sexual assault, and I'm a parent coach, helping them empower their kids to stay safe. So, when it comes to discussing abuse and danger, I'm considered an expert.

Finally (and most importantly), I raised two sons and am the doting grandma to three rapidly aging munchkins. When confronted with the simple innocence of my grandchildren, my experience helping thousands of crime victims was surprisingly unhelpful. Feeling utterly helpless, I asked, "How do I protect them?" More importantly, "How do I teach them to protect themselves?"

Researching and writing this and my other *Badass Parents* guides answered these questions and, in the process, can help YOU protect your loved ones too.

Why You Should Read This Book

Throughout your darling's childhood, she'll encounter tons of people—at school, during extracurricular activities, on outings with friends, and in your own home—most of whom you know fairly well. Yet any one of them could be a predator. I don't care how alert you think you are; you can't keep your kid in your sight every second. It's not possible, and it's not even remotely healthy.

Your child's best bet to stay safe is for you to teach her how to protect and defend herself when you're not around. By reading this book and following my advice, you're doing the most important thing you can do to protect your child from harm: *taking action*.

Research shows that kids taught to protect and defend themselves—by saying no, yelling, running away, or fighting—are less attractive to predators and stand a significantly greater chance of escaping an abusive situation or potential abduction.

Educating yourself and your child about body safety is super liberating. The seeds (the tips and tools I share) you plant in her mind today will blossom into positive behaviors that will serve her throughout her life. Rather than worrying about nebulous dangers, you'll know the facts. Once you teach your kid what I share in this book, you'll sleep better at night knowing you've taught her to be a mini badass who can stand up for herself.

As former slave and abolitionist Frederick Douglass observed (and I'm paraphrasing here), "It's far easier to raise strong children than to repair broken adults." I'm convinced that if I'd been taught that it was okay to say no in situations where I felt uncomfortable, 99 percent of the crappy things that happened to me as a kid and teenager would never have occurred, and I wouldn't have had to grapple with post-traumatic stress for most of my life.

By the way, if you're a survivor of child abuse, absolutely incorporate what you learn in this book into your parenting repertoire. It's your best chance to break the cycle! Be excited about having this opportunity to learn how to step up and protect your kid in a way you weren't.

What This Book Will Teach You

Before I began writing my *Badass Parenting* books, I surveyed parents, grandparents, and caregivers about their top concerns for their kids' safety, and the same questions kept cropping up. Here are the top five:

1. How do I teach my children about danger without scaring them to death?

2. What do I teach them so they know how to protect and defend themselves?

3. What are the signs that my child is being bullied or abused?

4. How do I get my kids to come to me if something happens to them?

5. How do I make them actually listen to me and apply what I teach them?

This book answers these questions and more so parents, grandparents, and caregivers can confidently empower their beloved tweens and teens.[iv]

Pardon Me While I Repeat Myself

This essential guide is a follow-up to my other books in this series for parents of kids 0 to 9—*Badass Parenting* and *Heroic Parenting*, both of which were published in 2020 (and became instant Amazon #1 bestsellers!). Because so much of the information I wrote back then is the same for tweens and teens, you'll find a lot of overlap between them.

Moving on.... Here's how this book is laid out:

First, I go deep and dark by addressing the dangers your kid faces head-on. In Part I on *Toxic People and How They Groom Kids*, I talk about the categories of predators that might have access to your child.

In Part II on *Where Danger Lurks*, I discuss bullying, cyberbullying and other online dangers, sexual abuse, and sex trafficking, including who the perps and victims tend to be and what to look out for. In this section, I added a lot more about online dangers (the area where crime is going up in a seriously bad way) and a new chapter on sex trafficking. Stick with me

---

iv If you have kids from 0 to 9, I hope you'll read either *Badass Parenting* (if you're comfortable with excessive and totally unnecessary profanity) or the PG-rated (but still somewhat irreverent) *Heroic Parenting*, both of which are available on Amazon.

through these heavy parts because it's essential information. The book gets MUCH lighter from there on out.

Next, I move you into the action sections, which are more fun and empowering, beginning with Part III on *What Your Kid Needs to Know*. This is where I tell you exactly what essential body safety skills you should teach your child. I also cover how to talk to your kid about sexual consent. Although this isn't a sex ed book, addressing consent is SUPER important, and I'll give you some ideas to help you ensure your kid knows how to navigate potentially loaded situations. In my humble opinion, this is THE most important chapter I've ever written, and it's an absolute must-read.

In Part IV, *Taking Your Kid to the Next Level*, I share ways to foster your child's confidence and self-esteem and teach her some serious verbal and physical moves she can use to avoid and escape dangerous situations. I also teach you how to talk about all this critical information through manageable, ongoing conversations and family meetings.

You'll notice that throughout the book, I refer you to the free bonus content on my website that'll take you deeper into the topics I cover. I'm constantly adding cool freebies and parenting hacks to my site, so visit often to see what's new and interesting.

What this book doesn't cover:
- Drug and alcohol abuse
- Hazing
- Gang violence
- Auto safety
- Firearm safety
- School shootings

I couldn't do it all, folks. There simply wasn't enough room to cover *every* danger your kid may encounter, and I'm not an expert in these areas. There are literally thousands of great books on these topics that you can buy online or in any bookstore.

For the Savvy Grandparents Who Are Reading This Book

Grandparents play a special role in the life of their grandchildren and can be a major source of wisdom and support. There are more than 2.4 million grandparents who are raising their grandkids.[19] If you're one of them, good on you! You're the one who's responsible for teaching your grandchildren the information I share in this book.

However, some grandparents refuse to believe their grandchildren's claims of abuse, especially if it happened at the hands of a parent, aunt, or uncle. No one wants to believe their own adult child could do such a thing, but it happens every day worldwide, and you need to believe your grandchild.

Believing and supporting him doesn't mean you don't love your own child who was the offender. It means you love them enough to get them the help they need to stop hurting children and, yes, to hold them accountable. If the abuser was a family member, you're in a unique position to stop the abuse, protect and support the victim, and ensure the perp never again has access to the victim.

Be there for your family. You're the matriarch/patriarch and can set the tone for how all this goes down.

Another great way to help your grandkids is to buy this book for your children who are themselves parents and ask them to read it and apply what they learn.

A Few Disclaimers

Every single chapter of this book could be a book unto itself. I've tried to give you the basics and encourage you to dive more deeply into whatever topics interest you. Under the Resources tab on my websitev, I list several excellent books, websites, and advocacy organizations; but the list is hardly comprehensive, so do your own homework to find other resources on the topics I cover here.

---

v www.cjscarlet.com/resources

Throughout this book, I mainly use the male pronoun to refer to predators because about 95 percent of perps are male. Women can and do perpetrate some sex crimes against children, but the numbers are very low. (Although, when it comes to physical abuse and neglect, women are even more likely than men to be the abusers. SMH)

I alternately use "she" and "he" when talking about your child, although I try not to switch the pronouns within sections to avoid giving you whiplash.

To be clear, when I talk about victim dynamics in this book, I'm in no way suggesting that being victimized is a failure on the part of the survivor. While some kids make better targets because they're vulnerable and/ or unprepared or unable to protect themselves, it's NEVER their fault. It's always the offenders' wrong actions that are to blame. Period.

Be sure to read the footnotes, which provide additional details you need to know and are occasionally funny.

The names of people featured in this book have been changed to protect their identities.

One final disclaimer: This book was written to help you teach your child to protect and defend herself. If you faithfully use the techniques within these pages, you'll help her minimize dangerous encounters and be safer. However, the advice found in *Raising Badass Kids* cannot protect every child in every situation. Use the ideas found here when you can, and always use your common sense and best judgment. You know your kid better than anyone and are the authority on what information she needs and can handle.

BE the parent your kid deserves!

Love,
Badass Grandma

PART I

Toxic People and How They Groom Kids

CHAPTER 1

The Skinny on Predators

There's a common saying—It's not what you know; it's *who* you know that counts.

This may be true when it comes to getting into a good school or securing a job, but I'm here to tell you it's *both* when it comes to predators. That's because WHAT you know about them can be your greatest defense.

As for the WHO? Knowing that predators look pretty much like everyone else and come from all walks of life may cause you to throw up your hands and ask, "Well then, who *can* I trust?"

The answer is, when it comes to your kid, *TRUST NO ONE.*

I'm not saying you need to be paranoid and think everyone is out to get your child. I *am* saying that you need to be vigilant about the people in your child's environment.

And, no, it's generally *not* strangers you need to be wary of. Most crimes committed against kids are by people they know… and they and you probably have trusted in the past. In fact, around 93 percent of crimes against kids are perpetrated by people known to them. For those of you who, like me, suck at math, that means just 7 percent of crimes against children are committed by strangers!

Who *Are* These People?

- Up to 95 percent of child sexual abusers are male.[20]
- Virtually all sexual predators are heterosexual, meaning they're not gay. In fact, 98 percent of male sexual abusers identify as heterosexual.[21] For

the people in the back (as in "back in the Stone Age"), sexual preference has *nothing* to do with pedophilia. Straight men who are pedophiles may molest boys as well as girls.

Likewise, transgender identity has absolutely nothing to do with sexual deviancy. Please understand this—the research doesn't bear out the idea that transgender people are often sexual predators in disguise. It's simply not true. However, transgender individuals are four times more likely to be the victims of sexual crimes.

- Predators can be single, married, or have kids of their own. Pedophiles may be in adult sexual relationships and still have a predilection for children.

- Contrary to what we see in movies, kidnappers and criminals don't always look sneaky, suspicious, or dangerous. They go to great lengths to appear as nice, respectable people. To a child's eye, they're exactly what a friendly and trustworthy adult would look like.

- On average, sex offenders begin molesting others by age 15 and molest an average of 117 children. Only rarely are these assaults reported.[22]

- The younger the victim, the more likely their abuser is a family member, including parents, guardians, stepparents, siblings, stepsiblings, cousins, uncles, aunts, and grandparents.

- Predators often have a strong sense of entitlement, believing life owes them something and that people exist for them to use and abuse. They lack empathy and don't care how their actions make their victims feel.

- They may have difficulty forming intimate relationships with other adults and choose to prey on kids because they can control them and feel powerful.

- They may have experienced a troubled childhood and/or sexual abuse (which is not an excuse that absolves their behavior!).

- They may abuse drugs or alcohol, which disinhibits them and numbs them to their actions when they abuse their victims. (Again, not an excuse.)

How Predators Groom Their Victims

Predators use grooming tactics to manipulate their victims and gain their trust. They're pros at quickly assessing the strengths and weaknesses of their chosen targets to decide which tactics will work best for each child.

Steve Kovacs, author of *Protect Your Kids! The Simple Keys to Children's Safety and Survival* writes that sexual predators choose kids who may crave attention, acceptance, love, or friendship. The child may have material needs, like the need for money, food, or clothes. Or he may covet luxury items, such as digital devices or electronic games.

Kovacs notes that pedophiles work hard to learn the names of popular rock or rap stars, the latest fashions, and which movie or TV stars their targets watch so they can be seen as cool and relatable. The perp will try to meet as many of the child's needs as possible, patiently plotting to assault him in the future.

When a predator showers a kid with attention and gifts, the child naturally feels grateful and may feel guilty if he doesn't reciprocate with affection or doesn't keep a secret for the predator.

What Grooming Looks Like

According to ChildLuresPrevention.com, "Early grooming efforts by sexual predators seek to determine if the child has a stable home life or if the family is facing challenges like poverty, divorce, illness, drugs, homelessness, etc. Children lacking stability at home are at higher risk for sexual abuse, as there is usually more access to the child and opportunities to abuse the child."[23]

Here are some grooming behaviors predators use that you should watch for:

- Seeking out children who lack self-confidence and have low self-esteem
- Targeting kids who aren't adequately supervised by their parents or other caregivers

- Spending time alone with kids, just hanging out or attending outings with them
- Giving gifts, favors, or special privileges
- Desensitizing kids to their touch by tickling, patting, stroking, or wrestling
- Isolating a child by spending a significant amount of time alone with him
- Hugging, kissing, and sharing other physical affection as a prelude to sexual contact
- Telling a kid to keep secrets
- Telling sexual jokes, showing pornography, or asking sexual questions
- Making the child feel responsible for any sexual misconduct that occurs

How Perps Gain Access to Their Victims

While some sexual abuse is purely opportunistic, most kids are groomed over time and lured into situations where they're vulnerable to abuse. Common grooming tactics include:[24]

- Befriending parents, particularly single parents, to gain access to their kids
- Offering babysitting services to busy parents or guardians
- Taking jobs or participating in community events that involve children
- Becoming a guardian, "Big Brother," or foster parent
- Attending kids' sporting events or offering to coach youth sports
- Volunteering in youth organizations
- Offering to chaperone overnight trips
- Loitering in places young people frequent—playgrounds, parks, malls, arcades, swimming pools, sports fields, etc.

- Befriending kids on social media (Snapchat, Instagram, Facebook, Tik Tok, etc.) and online gaming platforms

Predators' Favorite Targets

While all kids are vulnerable, approximately 20 percent of child sexual abuse victims are children under five, 50 percent are children between five and 12, and 30 percent are teens between 13 and 17.

Parents and guardians can help keep their kids safe by talking frankly and often with them about boundaries, sex, and consent. This is important to know: Convicted child molesters have admitted they're less likely to abuse kids with a basic understanding of sex education.

Some predators cite a preference for children on the brink of puberty. This is the age of sexual awakening, making it easy for molesters to prey on the sexual ignorance and curiosity of youngsters. To quote one sex offender, "Give me a kid who knows nothing about sex, and you've given me my next victim."

Child molesters will also target kids who are loners or look troubled or neglected. Young people who smoke, vape, or use drugs or alcohol are seen as risk-seekers lacking adequate supervision and may be seen as easy targets.

Sexual predators are *less likely* to abuse kids who have a basic understanding of sex education, know how to set and defend their boundaries, and say no to people who make them uncomfortable.

You're His Target Too!

Know this—predators don't just groom their victims. They may also groom *YOU*, the child's parent, and other family members and friends to gain your trust and greater access to your kid.

A predator does this by charming the adults in order to convince them he's a stand-up guy and role model. Many a perp has befriended a child's parents, particularly single moms, just to gain access to their kids. In some cases, pedophiles marry women to be their "beards"—their cover stories—

so people will think they're solid, upstanding citizens who can be trusted around kids.

Single moms are often targeted because they're more likely to be overwhelmed by parenting duties and vulnerable to offers to babysit and/or drive kids to school, practices, lessons, and other activities.

Outwitting Predators

Whether they're opportunistic criminals, power predators, or persuasion predators, perps usually have a plan for how they'll victimize your tween or teen. Your child's goal is to thwart them in as many ways as possible so the perp will decide she's a bad target and leave her alone.

Your kid can turn the tables on a potential predator by being alert to his charm offensive. If she's paying close attention to what the predator is saying and doing, he might reveal clues that will tip her off to his motives and, therefore, his potential for trying to commit an assault. She should be aware of her surroundings and level of comfort with him. If she finds herself in a situation with someone she doesn't know or trust, she should be alert to cues from her intuition that signal this person is a potential threat and get away from him as quickly as possible.

Predators are always assessing others to find potential victims. The stronger and more confident your child appears, the less appealing she'll look to them. Awareness equals greater security!

I'll take a hit on this from people who say the responsibility shouldn't be on kids to alter their behavior to avoid victimization. I completely agree! However, this is the real world we live in, and until people no longer treat children—girls in particular—as objects, toys, or victims, we need to be practical.

Please, please tell your kid not to put herself in harm's way because she's too embarrassed to ask someone to walk her to her car after work or too proud to admit that she's too impaired by drugs or alcohol to function.

It's common sense; if your tween or teen chooses to engage in high-risk behavior, she's a more attractive target for predators. High-risk behavior consists of anything she does that compromises her safety, whether it's going for a walk on the beach with the cute guy she just met at a party or drinking so much that she's not in control anymore.

Don't be afraid to ask your kid if anyone has asked her to keep secrets, which the predator may use to test and control her. For example, the perp may give your child money when she visits and warn her not to tell you or she'll get in trouble. This secret creates a bond between them and acts as a "feeler," meaning he's testing her willingness to keep a secret so he can escalate his behavior later.

Some perps skip over the charm offensive and threaten your child that if she doesn't keep his assaults a secret, he'll hurt her or her siblings, friends, pets, or even you, the parent. He may also use shame and guilt to keep your kid from revealing the abuse, telling her that she'll get in trouble or be blamed for what happened.

Dirtbag move, I know, but VERY effective.

Sadly, some predators manipulate their targets so thoroughly that the victims may believe the predator genuinely loves them. In return, they develop strong, loving feelings and come to depend on their abusers. This is especially common in cases such as child sexual abuse involving a parent. If the child is emotionally and physically dependent on the predator, it's easy to fall into his trap, and it becomes more difficult to resist or report him.

Again, to be clear, *I am NOT blaming the victim!* There exists a power dynamic that may lead some kids to become codependent because they believe it's the safest or most loving course of action. But it's never the child's fault if she's victimized; it's a choice the predator makes and forces upon her.

What Predators Really Want

Bottom line: Predators have only one interest—to satisfy their need for power, control, or sexual satisfaction. They enjoy their victims' response to the acts as much as the acts themselves. They're seeking kids who respond as they desire—either by fighting, which allows the predators to overpower them, or by complying, which enables the predators to complete their assaults without resistance.

When someone assaults a child, it's usually about control—of her behavior, body, emotions, or boundaries. Predators usually begin by taking charge of little things, such as running the conversation or telling inappropriate jokes to gauge your kid's reaction. They'll move on to increasingly invasive behavior if she doesn't object. Their actions could escalate quickly and start with the predator violating the child's personal space or cornering her in an isolated location.

Predators are also on the lookout for the means to commit their crimes. They may watch your child closely for some time, from minutes to months. They may seek out weapons they can use to threaten her. They're always looking for the best locations to position her that offer the greatest secrecy and ability to flee quickly and easily. They're counting on her to be terrified and compliant.

Above all, predators want victims who won't report the crime, and they'll often threaten their targets to keep them silent, telling them they'll harm them or their families. They may also use the children's own shame and guilt to keep them from talking, for example, by telling the kids they'll get in trouble or be blamed for what happened.

What Predators *Don't* Want

The number one thing predators don't want is to get caught, especially if they plan to use a weapon, which results in longer prison sentences if they're convicted. This is their biggest fear. Use it against them!

Predators are likely to be deterred:

- When your kid walks confidently and with purpose.
- When she takes up as much space as possible. Holding her chin up and standing tall make her appear strong and likely to resist an attack.
- When she pays attention to where she is and what's going on around her. Talking or playing on her cell phone makes your kid MORE, not less, vulnerable. Although talking to her friend or parent on her phone

when she's walking to school may make her feel safer, it actually puts her at greater risk of being attacked. And really, what are you, the parent, supposed to do if she's attacked while you're talking to her? You're basically helpless and can't even call the police if you're not in the same 911 jurisdiction. If she wants reassurance, have her carry a personal security device and keep it in her hand (it does her no good if it's sitting in the bottom of her backpack!).

- When she makes eye contact to show the perp she's paying attention, which makes the predator nervous, knowing she could identify him in a lineup. She shouldn't stare him down, though; just look him over so he knows she sees him.

- When she sets firm boundaries. Telling someone to back off or leave her alone shows that she has strong boundaries and is willing to defend herself. Also, telling someone to stop making inappropriate comments or jokes sends the message that she won't tolerate bad behavior.

- When she resists the perp's commands by running away or fighting back if she can do so. This is especially important if the predator tries to move her to another location.

- When she uses the rabid Tasmanian devil fighting moves I teach in Chapter 14 or gets formal self-defense or martial arts training (*and* becomes proficient through regular practice) that prepares her to fight off an attacker.

- When she uses personal security products or weapons to help defend herself (which can be purchased on my merch site at https://www.mydamselpro.net/cjscarlet).

- When she reports the predator to parents and the police. Predators hate that!

Badass Grandma's Two Cents

My top takeaways:

- I just can't emphasize it enough—sexual predators are less likely to abuse kids who have a basic understanding of sex education, know how to set and defend their boundaries, and say no to people who make them uncomfortable.

- Predators don't just groom their victims; they may also groom YOU, the child's parent, and other family members and friends to gain your trust and greater access to your kid.
- Your child—and YOU!—have more power to protect him than you may think. By reading this book and teaching him what I share, you help your kid become a bad target for predators.

In the remaining chapters in Part I, I go into greater depth on the exact types of predators out there so you can be more aware and vigilant when your kid is exposed to people in these categories.

You're doing great! Keep reading.

CHAPTER 2

Stranger Danger? Not So Fast!

The 99.999+ Percent

I'm going to blow a few minds here by saying that teaching your child to fear strangers by harping about "stranger danger" is, well, downright dangerous.

Virtually 100 percent of the world is made up of people your kid doesn't know, and nearly every one of those 8 billion people *pose absolutely no threat to him*. In fact, strangers make up just seven percent of perpetrators! The other 93 percent are someone your child knows.

Kids often believe strangers look "different" (in a strange way) from people they know. For example, in the HBO special *How to Raise a Street-Smart Child*,[vi] the children featured thought a stranger was someone who appeared threatening and evil and looked "mean and ugly." In fact, predators look pretty much like everyone else.

Teaching your kid that strangers shouldn't be trusted can cause him to feel anxious and afraid when he encounters people he hasn't met before, and it can lead him to automatically trust people he knows who may actually pose a threat.

Okay, so now that we're being more realistic about the infinitesimally small possibility that a complete stranger will abuse your darling child, let's explore why teaching him how to interact with strangers is important.

---

vi This movie is a bit dated, having been released in 1987, but according to my experience, today's kids are just as naive.

Everyone Is a Stranger Until They're Not

Everyone we've ever met was once a stranger—even our parents. Your kid will meet thousands of people in his lifetime. A few of them will be truly bad, but most of them will be good.

And guess what? Most of the time, you won't be there to help him figure out who to trust and who to avoid. It's way better to teach your kid from the time he's young how to use his intuition to assess whether that stranger (and even those he knows well) feels and acts like a safe person.

If you really want your kid not to go anywhere with anyone—stranger or otherwise—without your express permission, teach him THAT, rather than scaring him into believing all strangers are dangerous.

Again, everyone's a stranger at first, and your child needs to learn how to use his intuition to put people into the "safe" or "unsafe" categories so he knows who to be on guard around and who to avoid completely.

Teaching your tween or teen how to discern whom to trust takes time and ongoing conversations, which I'll cover next.

People-Watching

One fun way to teach your kid to differentiate between safe and unsafe people is to people-watch. You can do this with your tween or teen anytime, anywhere.

Simply watch the people around you and talk about them. C'mon, you know you do it anyway! Just tweak your comments a bit from being purely catty to being open and observant about the clues others are sending out through their appearance and behavior.

This exercise aims to teach your kid how to critically observe people for signs that they appear unsafe. As you and your child watch people and talk about your impressions of them, make it clear that he should mainly focus on their actions and body language, looking for clues that a particular person deserves extra scrutiny and caution. For example, help him note when someone looks angry or aggressive, which may indicate a controlling or volatile personality, or if he feels weirded out by someone who leers at women or kids as they walk by.

By closely watching people's behavior, your kid will learn that just because someone's wearing a suit doesn't automatically mean he's trustworthy, any more than a person wearing a hoodie and sporting multiple body piercings means she's dangerous. Put simply, it's how a person makes your child *feel* that counts the most, and you should validate those feelings when he shares them. Talk about the clues he picked up on that prompted those feelings.

Use role-playing to help your kid think through how he would react if he was approached by one of those people. You can say, "I can see why that person makes you feel uncomfortable. I sense that too. If he tried to talk to you and you felt uncomfortable, you could say, 'My mom's waiting for me. I have to go.' Or, if he was making you feel afraid, you could even yell for me and run away as fast as you can to a safe person or place."

Let your kid think through what he would do in each situation. Listen to his full answer and validate his impressions. If necessary, help him tweak his responses to ensure they're on target.

People-watching with your kid will help him feel greater confidence when encountering strangers, knowing he can trust himself to know when someone or something doesn't feel right and that he has the right and the power to take steps to avoid them.

Who Should Your Kid Trust?

If your child felt uncomfortable or in danger around someone, would he know whom to approach for help? Many parents tell their kids to find a police officer, but the chances of one being close by at that exact moment are virtually nonexistent. You could also encourage your kid to look for a store clerk wearing a badge or vest, but these people may be hard to spot.

If your kid doesn't immediately see a police officer or store clerk, teach him to look for a woman, preferably with children or one who's older, and ask her for help. As we've learned, women are far less likely to be predators and more likely to help him.

Remind your kid that before approaching anyone, woman, police offi-cer, or clerk, he should watch them carefully for a moment and check in with his intuition about whether they feel "safe."

Badass Grandma's Two Cents

My top takeaways:

1. If you really want your child not to go anywhere with anyone—stranger or otherwise—without your express permission, teach him THAT, rather than scaring him into believing all strangers are dangerous.

2. Most of the time, you won't be there to help your kid figure out who to trust and who to avoid. It's way better to teach him from the time he's young how to use his intuition to assess whether that stranger (and even those he knows well) feels and acts like a safe person.

3. Everyone's a stranger at first, and your kid needs to learn how to use his intuition to put people into the "safe" or "unsafe" categories, so he knows who to be on guard around and who to avoid completely.

Now that we're clear on the fallacy of "stranger danger," in the next chapter, I'll focus on people your child knows and interacts with regularly who are more likely to pose a threat.

CHAPTER 3

Juvenile Sex Offenders

Shockingly, more than one-third of reported sex offenses against young people are committed by other kids.[25]

The media and internet are rife with stories of entitled young men sexually assaulting or raping their peers. Appallingly, these crimes are too often not reported, or the perpetrators aren't charged, or they're given a laughably light sentence when they're found guilty. (Unless they're Black and poor, in which case, they're more likely to receive lengthy sentences.)

But other cases involving child-on-child sex offenses are rarely mentioned in the media (mostly because they're seldom reported). And yet it happens all the time.

When Sexual Experimentation Becomes a Crime

The general rule for sexual activity between kids is that if they're within three years of age of each other, are similar in size and emotional development, *and it's mutually acceptable to both of them; it's* considered normal sexual experimentation (child's play).

But when the behavior involves kids who are farther apart in age, size, or emotional maturity, or when one child is being forced to participate or is being sexually assaulted, it's considered abuse and may even constitute a criminal offense.

And that can be far more egregious than most people imagine. While statutes vary by state, the National Sex Offender Registration and Notification Act requires juveniles convicted of aggravated sexual abuse crimes or rape to register as sex offenders. In at least one case, a 10-year-old child was convicted of sexually assaulting five younger boys and had to register as a sex offender for the rest of his life.

This is serious shit, people.

Who the Juvenile Offenders Are

People don't morph into predators the minute they turn 18. Many of them start abusing others when they're kids themselves. Twenty-three percent of these young offenders are just 10 to 12 years old, and 70 percent are under 16.[26] Most target other kids who are younger than they are.

Juveniles who commit child-on-child sexual abuse are more likely than adults to do the following:[27]

- Offend in groups with one or more co-offenders (24 percent for juveniles versus 14 percent for adults)
- Offend at a school (12 percent versus 2 percent)
- Commit sodomy[vii] (13 percent versus 7 percent) and fondling (49 percent versus 42 percent)
- Target children under 12 (59 percent of juvenile offenders versus 39 of adult offenders)
- Victimize males (25 percent versus 13 percent)

Studies show that between 40 to 80 percent of youths who sexually molest or assault other kids have themselves been sexually abused and that 20 to 50 percent have been physically abused.[28]

Regardless of the reason, abuse and assault by a peer or sibling can be just as frightening and traumatizing as abuse by an adult.

Who the Victims Are

Eighteen percent of girls and 3 percent of boys say that by age 17, they had been victims of sexual assault or abuse at the hands of another youth. Fifteen percent of these incidents involved penetration.[29]

---

vii Sodomy generally refers to oral and anal sex acts.

Eighty-four percent of the victims of other kids were under the age of 12.[30] Ninety-four percent of victims knew the juvenile offender.[31]

The Dirty Little Secret No One Wants to Talk About— Abuse Between Siblings

The majority (69 percent) of sex offenses committed by juveniles occur in the home—and by "the home," I mean potentially *your* home.[32] When the offender is a sibling, the child victim is at greater risk of repeat abuse because she's constantly exposed to her perpetrator. In fact, sibling sexual abuse is significantly more common than parental sexual abuse and is often more intrusive and occurs over longer periods.[33]

That's worth repeating to make sure you heard me—*sibling sexual abuse is significantly more common than parental sexual abuse*. Got it? Good.

Sexual abuse by a sibling, a form of incest, can be traumatic and emotionally devastating for a child and haunt her throughout her life. Victims are known for blaming themselves and feeling they somehow did something to cause it to happen or "asked for it"—by not saying no, being "too pretty," not resisting, initially enjoying it, etc.

The buried trauma can cause survivors to experience long-term mental health problems, trouble forming healthy relationships, sexual dysfunction, and other symptoms of post-traumatic stress.

When child victims tell on their abusive sibling—which isn't often—some parents are supportive and proactive, work to stop the abuse, and get counseling for both kids. Sadly, it seldom plays out that way. More often, parents react with shock, disbelief, or denial, which can further enable the abuse. It's very rare for parents to report their abusive child to the authorities.

There aren't many things worse than learning one of your kids is molesting or even sexually assaulting one of your other children. But if you think or know that one child is being abused by another, you *must* act as quickly to ensure the victim's safety in the home and get immediate help from a professional counselor for both kids (who will have separate appointments, obviously).

Abusive Dating Relationships

Does your kid know the difference between "love" and abuse? Do you? Would you recognize the signs that your tween or teen is in an abusive relationship? If you answered yes, know that research suggests otherwise.

Eighty-one percent of parents surveyed said they believe teen dating violence is not an issue or admit they didn't know if it's an issue.[34] And although 82 percent of parents felt confident they could tell if their kid was experiencing dating abuse, a majority (58 percent) couldn't correctly identify all the warning signs of abuse.[35]

I hate to do it, but I'm going to give you more scary statistics to get your attention and make you take seriously the possibility that your child could be vulnerable to dating violence:

- Intimate partner violence against young women between 16 and 24 is *almost triple* that of older adults.[36]

- Violent adolescent relationships put the victims at higher risk for substance abuse, eating disorders, risky sexual behavior, and further partner violence.[37]

- Teen girls who've been physically or sexually abused are six times more likely to become pregnant and twice as likely to contract a sexually transmitted disease.[38]

- Fifty percent (*yes, half!*) of young people who've been victims of dating violence and rape have considered or attempted suicide, compared to 12.5 percent of non-abused girls and 5.4 percent of non-abused boys.[39]

Emily Rothman, an associate professor of community health sciences at Boston University School of Public Health, stated, "I've been amazed at how little some [students] know about what counts as abusive behavior. There are people who don't realize, for example, that breaking into your partner's phone and snooping through their texts counts as controlling, abusive, illegal behavior."

Rothman and fellow researcher Megan Bair-Merritt noted that abuse can start as early as age 11 and can range from physical violence and sexual exploitation to controlling intimidation and hurtful mind games. They also found that partner violence can be difficult to recognize and stop because it can come from many directions—in person or online—and can involve a current dating partner or someone from a former relationship.[40]

Sadly, girls as young as middle-school age feel like the world will end if they don't have a boyfriend. This desperation makes them vulnerable to abusers who seek someone to dominate and control. Kids often confuse controlling behavior, such as constant checking on their activities and relationships, for closeness and caring.

It's not just partner violence that can confuse young minds; the line between sexual intimacy and rape can also be blurred. Two older surveys (from 1988 and 1998, which I'm including for the shock value) of sixth- through ninth-grade students conducted by the Rhode Island Rape Crisis Center found that *many young people believe forced sex is acceptable under some circumstances.* (Italics are mine.)

The survey of boys and girls ages 11 to 14 found that half thought forced sex was acceptable if the boy "spent a lot of money" on the girl. Sixty-five percent of boys and 47 percent of girls said it was acceptable for a boy to rape a girl if they've been dating for more than six months. And 87 percent of boys and 79 percent of girls said sexual assault was acceptable if the man and woman were married.[41]

How messed up is THAT?!

Although teenage girls are the most likely to be victimized, they're the least likely to report it when assaulted. Having just been given permission to date, they may be reluctant to tell their parents when their date or boyfriend is abusive because they fear they won't be allowed to date anymore. In truth, telling you (the parent) when she's in danger shows that she has enough maturity and judgment to make good relationship choices.

As her parent, you should ask lots of questions to gauge the health and safety of your child's new relationships. If you suspect she's in an abusive relationship or may have been sexually assaulted, don't hesitate to talk with her to discover the truth. Chances are, she's dying to talk to someone she can trust but is afraid of getting in trouble herself.

If Your Child Is the Offender

Please visit my website at www.cjscarlet.com/freebies/ for an article on what to do if you discover your child is sexually molesting or assaulting another person.

Badass Grandma's Two Cents

My top takeaways:

1. More than one-third of reported sex offenses against kids are committed by other kids, with the majority (69 percent) committed by siblings in the home.

2. Sibling sexual abuse is significantly more common than parental sexual abuse and is often more intrusive and occurs over longer periods.

3. Teen girls who've been physically or sexually abused are *six times* more likely to become pregnant and twice as likely to contract a sexually transmitted disease.

So, so many inappropriate incidents between kids could be avoided if they're taught about consent and how to navigate it. I'll cover this in depth in Chapter 10. PLEASE read that chapter and teach your kid what you learn there to help him avoid becoming a victim or perpetrator! Better yet, let your kid read that chapter himself (or read it together) and then talk about what he learned.

CHAPTER 4

All in the Family

Incest.

Blech! The word is universally reviled and so far "out there" that some people literally shudder when they hear it.

Incest is defined as sexual relations or abuse perpetrated by someone who's considered a family member—whether they're biologically related or not. Incestuous behavior includes:

- Having a child pose or perform in a sexual fashion, or when an offender does the same in front of the child
- Peeping or spying on the child
- Having the child view sexual acts in person, in movies, or in magazines
- Having explicit sexual conversations with the child
- Sexual touching
- Sexual assault (which can include sodomy or rape)

There are disagreements between sociologists about whether the prohibition against incest is innate or socialized; regardless, it's perceived by virtually every culture on the planet as unnatural and emotionally traumatizing behavior.

Of course, any form of abuse or assault can be traumatic to the victims, but incest is often worse because the perpetrators are people the victims love most and may rely on for their survival and welfare. They're the people the kids should be able to trust the most. When that trust is violated, it creates a deep moral wound that can cause lasting psychological harm, impairing their ability to lead a normal, healthy life.

I'll talk about the short- and long-term effects of sexual abuse in Chapter 8. For now, let's look at who the familial offenders are.

The Call Is Coming from *Inside the House!* When the Abuser Is Your Partner

For many parents, learning their child has been sexually molested or assaulted is about as bad as it gets. But it can get even worse if the abuser is someone the parent is in an intimate relationship with.

Children who live with their married biological parents experience the lowest rates of abuse and neglect, while those living with a single parent with a live-in partner (about a third of all children) are *20 times more likely to be sexually abused.*[42]

You read that right. Kids living with a single parent and their non-related live-in partner are 20 times more likely to be sexually abused than their peers in two-parent families. They're also *100 times more likely to be killed by a stepfather than by a biological parent*, according to Gavin De Becker.

What the hell is *that* all about?

It may be because people who aren't biologically related to the children don't feel an emotional connection to them. Also, surrogate parents may be less able to convince the kids to obey them and resort to psychological control or physical force to exert control over them.

Sociologists argue about the causes behind this "Cinderella effect." The solutions they propose basically involve completely altering societal realities and family dynamics. Their suggestions are well-meaning but unrealistic because people are people, and some people just suck!

Seriously, there will always be buttheads in our world who are driven, for whatever reason, to hurt other people. The purpose of *this* book is to prepare you and your child to live in a world with those kinds of people

38

and still come out unscathed because you both learned to protect and defend yourself from said buttheads.

Things That Make You Go, "WTH?"

As I mentioned earlier, some sexual predators marry women either to use them as their "beards"—meaning they use the marriage to appear normal and respectable while they're actually busy molesting kids—or to gain access to kids (theirs through marriage or their partner's) they can victimize.

My former brother-in-law, who was a classic pedophile, used my sister this way. He married her and they had four children, but my sister always sensed that he barely tolerated her from the get-go. He was a normal father in some ways—he spent time with his kids, helped with their homework, cooked most of their meals, and did all the usual dad stuff. But he also molested several kids (both boys and girls) over the years. He was ultimately arrested and charged with child sexual abuse but committed suicide the day the trial was to begin. True story.

Other men enter into relationships with women who already have children just to gain access to their kids. They can be extremely charming to both the women and their kids—grooming the whole family—all while plotting to molest the kids as soon as they can.

I urge everyone who's thinking about dating, moving in with, or marrying another person—man or woman—to do a background check on them first. Maybe even hire a private investigator to ensure they're everything they claim to be.

"*Wha??? But that's... so... so... underhanded!*" you argue. "*I couldn't possibly spy on my boyfriend!*" you cry. "*I don't want him to think I don't trust him!*" you bleat.

Get over yourself. This is about the safety and well-being of your kid (or future kid if you don't have any yet). You should do at least as much research on someone who may become your child's caregiver as you do, say, figuring out which streaming TV service to buy.

I can't tell you how many women I've helped over the years whose partners turned out to be terrible, abusive jerks whose backgrounds were a total effing lie—something they would have discovered in minutes if they'd invested any time looking into their backgrounds. A good background check service only costs around $20 and will tell you if the person you're researching has any criminal convictions or is on the National Sex Offender Registry (searches of the registry are free).[viii]

But don't rely just on a background search. After all, the person may never have been caught and convicted, so there won't be a record. An intuitive hit is your most important clue; *trust it.*

Soooo many people have nagging feelings they can't quite silence, no matter how hard they try, that whisper to them something's not right about the person they're dating or living with or have already married. They tell themselves it's nothing, that they're imagining things or being overly sensitive when their partner does something douchey. They squelch that sick feeling in the pit of their stomach when they see the creepy way their partner smiles when he looks at their kids.

But deep in their hearts and guts, they *know* something's wrong. They just don't want to consciously admit it because it would mean they'd have to end the relationship. *And that's SO hard!* (Yes, I'm being sarcastic.)

My advice? Suck it up, buttercup. If your gut sends you distress signals (no matter how minuscule) that something's off with a person you're seeing, stop seeing them.

Yes, it's that simple.

Your gut knows things your mind hasn't noticed yet, and it'll never steer you wrong. Trust it, and you'll avoid months or years of torment, regret, and therapy bills for you and your kid.

---

viii Please be sure you're looking up the right person. Use the correct spelling of their full name and any aliases they use (as well as name variations they may use—e.g., "Jimmy" and "Jimmie"), and their address and birthdate to help you narrow the search to the right individual. And don't forget to check the National Sex Offender Registry for their name. You don't want to base your decisions on information about the wrong person!

Even if everything seems hunky-dory with your new love, spring for the 20 bucks and do a background check anyway. To quote Forest Gump quoting his mother: "Life is like a box of chocolates; you never know what you're gonna get." Could be nothing, could be something. Either way, you'll feel better knowing you took action.

The Call Is Coming From *Outside the House,* and It's Your Ex on the Line

It never ceases to amaze me how much people can come to absolutely *loathe* the partner they used to think hung the moon once they believe that person is no longer meeting their needs or has thwarted them in some way.

Think about it. If you're willing to be totally honest with yourself, when you look back at your former relationships, you'll find that your feelings toward your mate changed only after they DIDN'T DO something you WANTED, or they DID something you DIDN'T WANT.

Do you see it yet? C'mon, you have to be brutally honest here!

Whatever the reason you broke up with a past partner, if you have a kid together you're bound to each other until the child is at least 18. Hopefully, for the child's sake, you both play nice.

But what do you do when your former partner is abusing your child? *You do whatever it takes to protect your child*, short of breaking the law or kidnapping her yourself.

If you think your kid has been physically or sexually abused by your ex (or anyone else, for that matter), there are several things you should do:

- If your child returns from visiting your ex-partner with injuries, take her to a hospital immediately. Her immediate safety and well-being are your most pressing concern.

- Next, call your local child protective or social services agency and report the abuse. They'll investigate the case and arrange professional help for your child.

- If there's a court visitation order in place, contact the court immediately and ask for an immediate hearing to temporarily revoke visita-

41

tion or provide for visitation with supervision until the investigation is over.

- Contact your local child advocacy center, which can help you navigate the social services and criminal justice systems and provide counseling for your child.[ix]

- Sit down and thoroughly document what you know and/or have witnessed [e.g., bruises or other injuries to the child after a visit to your ex-partner, symptoms of sexual abuse (which I detail in Chapter 8), statements she's made about being fearful or hurt by your ex, etc.). Include as much detail as you can, such as dates, times, and locations. This will bolster your claims and provide social workers and the courts with a timeline of events.

A Cautionary Note on Using Children as Pawns

When I was the executive director of a child advocacy center in the mid-'90s, I witnessed some of the most horrible child abuse cases imaginable... some of which *never actually happened*. You see, they were cases in which separated or divorced parents manipulated the system to punish and/or attempt to control each other by using their children as pawns, claiming the other parent was abusing them.

Whether it involves a contentious custody case or "just" a vindictive act of revenge to get back at one's ex, this is *despicable* behavior. Don't play that game. If it's being done to you, lawyer up (the best you can) and fight it! But whatever you do, don't retaliate in kind. Your soul and your child's happiness and mental health are on the line here.

Other Relatives as Threats

There's such a thing as too much family closeness. Relatives tend to have more access to kids than others, and access is the most obvious thing someone needs to abuse a child. I myself was molested by a brother-in-law

---

ix ChildHelp.org's National Child Abuse Hotline number is 800-422-4453.

and, in one particularly horrific incident, by a drunken uncle within hours of his wife's funeral. Another true story.

Many parents who are suspicious of other adults are often oblivious and even careless when their kids are around relatives. Most families have a handsy, slightly rapey "funny uncle" that everyone knows to avoid. But, just as teenagers WILL find a time and place to canoodle despite your best efforts to chaperone them, sure as shootin' that funny uncle will find a way to be alone with your kid.

If you have any inkling that one of your relatives poses a threat to your child (or any child), the only way to ensure your son or daughter's safety is to prevent them from being in that person's presence. *Cut off the access and you eliminate the threat.*[x]

Now, what about the ones who aren't so overtly pervy? Well, most of the time when we tell ourselves we had no idea Uncle Teddy was "like that," there were actually glaring clues that he was. Read some of the telling signs below. When you observe any of these, take my advice and cut off all access to that person who makes you or your child go, "ick."

Again, I turn to author Steve Kovacs, who warns parents to be especially wary of someone who:[43]

- Spends a suspiciously large amount of time with children or a particular child
- Makes sexual jokes or comments or talks about sexual activities with or around children
- Calls kids names with a sexual overtone (e.g., slut, whore, stud, etc.)
- Is overly complimentary about a child's appearance
- Looks at or talks about child pornography (this may constitute a federal crime)

---

x Many states have mandatory reporting laws that require every adult to report suspected abuse. If you know or suspect that a child is being or has been abused by ANYONE, report it to the police immediately (you may be able to do so anonymously).

- Tells kids to keep secrets and not tell anyone about certain activities
- Is overly affectionate with kids, including too much hugging, kissing, tickling, wrestling, holding them on their lap, or other touching, especially if they continue even when the child tells them to stop
- Walks in on kids in the bathroom or bedroom more often than could be chalked up to an "accident"
- Becomes defensive when asked about a child's health or gives conflicting stories about injuries to the child

Badass Grandma's Two Cents

My key takeaways:

1. Children who live with their married biological parents experience the lowest rates of abuse and neglect, while those living with a single parent with a live-in partner (about a third of all children) are *20 times more likely to be sexually abused.*

2. Your gut knows things your mind hasn't noticed yet, and it'll never steer you wrong. Trust it when it warns you that something—or someone—isn't right, and you'll avoid months or years of torment, regret, and therapy bills for you and your kid.

If your kid tells you he's been sexually abused by someone in your family or even that he's just uncomfortable around them, you *must* take action to protect him from further harm. Yes, that may mean reporting the perp to the police and social services, and yes, it may tear your family apart, but would you prefer to live a life of complete denial and face the roaring flames of eternal damnation, or do the adult thing and protect your child and family? *Hmmm?*

This particular scenario happens more often than not: A kid (or grown adult who was molested as a child) summons the courage to tell his parents that a relative abused him, *and the parent doesn't believe him and does NOTHING about it!*

I'm serious; I've heard this story from way too many adult survivors whose parents simply didn't want to believe that Aunt Lulu would do such a thing.

Don't be that parent. Just... don't.

CHAPTER 5

When Authority Figures Abuse Their Power

As parents, we rely on other adults to help us raise our kids and mold them into responsible people. Every day we hand our children off to teachers, coaches, scoutmasters, doctors, or religious figures. Nearly all these people will be safe, but some of them won't and we need to be on the lookout for threats.

Human beings tend to get full of themselves when they're put in positions of power. To paraphrase Sir John Dalberg-Acton, "Power corrupts; absolute power corrupts absolutely." Most of the time that manifests as irritating douchebaggery, but sometimes it leads people to believe they can use and abuse others, including innocent kids.

Whenever there's an imbalance of power, as there is between your child and any older youth or adult leader of a class, group, team, or religious institution, those in charge may feel powerful and entitled—a bad combination that may lead them to abuse their charges without compunction.

Teach your kid that just because he respects or even reveres someone doesn't mean he has to let his guard down or ignore his intuition. Occasionally ask your child, "What does your gut say about so and so?" This will cause him to start paying attention and teach him to automatically check in with his intuition, especially when interacting with new people.

Check to see if the school or organization conducts background checks on their employees and volunteers. If not, do your own background check on anyone who will regularly interact with your child. It's only around $20 for an individual search and $30 a month for unlimited searches, depending on the service you choose.

Note: Know that you may need the person's permission first before you can do a background search on them. If they refuse to give their permission, that's a sign they're not to be trusted. Don't let them anywhere near your kid.

Not the Kind of Schooling You Want

An estimated 4.5 million K-12 students have experienced inappropriate behavior by a teacher or other school official, including lewd comments, exposure to pornography, peeping, and grabbing. And three million students have experienced sexual touching or full-on assault.[44]

Here's a breakdown of school employees who have assaulted students:[45]

- 31 percent were teachers or substitutes
- 15 percent were coaches
- 12 percent were bus drivers
- 11 percent were teacher's aides
- 10 percent were security guards
- 6 percent were principals
- 5 percent were counselors (seriously?)
- The remaining 10 percent were other school employees

The most recent study of teacher-student sexual abuse commissioned by the U.S. Department of Education found that up to seven percent of all middle and high school students were the targets of physical sexual abuse by teachers, coaches, and other adults working in the school system. These statistics put the number of young teens sexually abused by teachers and other school adults *in the millions.*

These incidents have very serious implications, not only for the sexual, emotional, and mental health of the victims but also for their academic success as well. Another survey, *America After 3PM*, conducted by the

Afterschool Alliance and JC Penney Afterschool, found that students who experienced some form of abuse by teachers and other school employees reported they:

- Felt embarrassed, self-conscious, and less confident
- Felt afraid
- Felt confused about their sexual identity
- Doubted whether they could have a happy romantic relationship
- Tried to avoid the abuser
- Didn't want to go to school
- Had difficulty paying attention in and out of class
- Stayed home from school or cut class
- Found it hard to study
- Experienced health effects, including trouble sleeping and loss of appetite
- Experienced academic or disciplinary repercussions
- Scored a lower grade on a test or assignment
- Felt less likely to get a good grade
- Changed schools

Teachers and Professors

Sexual abuse happens in all grades, with 56 percent occurring during middle or high school. Most of this abuse occurs in the school—in empty classrooms, in hallways, in offices. Sometimes the abuse even happens right in front of other students!

According to a leadership and policy study on educator sexual abuse, just 6 percent of students report sexual abuse by a teacher or other staff member to someone who can do something about it. The others don't tell anyone. Or they talk to a friend about it and then swear the friend to secrecy.[46]

When students do tell, they almost always confide incidents of contact sexual abuse (touching, kissing, hugging, or forced intercourse), while verbal and visual abuse (e.g., where the perp exposes their genitals) are rarely reported to school officials.[47]

In many school districts, teachers are exempt from fingerprint and background check regulations. Even when students make a report and the district responds, law enforcement is rarely notified. As a result, most cases are not logged into the criminal justice system and the incidents are dealt with only at the school level, if at all.

It's important to note that kids who are taught about preventing sexual abuse at school are more likely to tell an adult if they experience it. Talking to your kid really does work!

Coaches

Over a 15-year period, Jerry Sandusky, an assistant football coach at Penn State, molested numerous boys whom he met mainly through a nonprofit that worked to provide care to foster children.[xi]

One of the biggest coaching sex abuse scandals in youth athletics in recent years continues to involve USA Swimming. So far, over a hundred coaches working for USA Swimming's member clubs have been permanently banned from the sport for molesting, groping, and secretly filming the young athletes under their care.

In the United Kingdom, a 2015 study found that 75 percent of youth athletes in organized sports experienced psychological/emotional abuse,[48] which the International Olympic Committee names as the "gateway" to other forms of non-accidental violence.[49]

Abuse in the sports environment can include physical abuse, neglect, emotional or psychological abuse, sexual abuse, or rape by a coach or staff member, as well harassment or abuse by peers.

While the warning signs below don't always indicate abuse, they DO cross the boundary between student-athletes and coaches:

---

xi I don't know how some people live with themselves. SMH

- Spending one-on-one time with kids, such as in private practice sessions or on overnight trips
- Touching kids in ways not related to or necessary for training
- Singling out a child for special attention or giving him gifts
- Telling sexual or inappropriate jokes or stories to a child
- Commenting on a child's appearance when not related to the sport

Scoutmasters, Other Group Leaders, and Volunteers

Here's another seriously disturbing fact: Nearly 90 percent of youth organizations don't conduct any type of criminal records check on volunteers and almost half don't even check their references! At the same time, some organizations want to ban gay people from being volunteers because they falsely believe they're more likely to abuse children.[xii]

As for the victims of group leader and volunteer abuse, it's impossible to reliably estimate how many there are out there. Very few cases are ever reported, and in only a fraction of those is action taken to prosecute the abuser. Instead, rather than firing the abusers, organizations (I'm looking at you, Boy Scouts and churches!) often choose to move the alleged perps to other troops or parishes where they're free to molest even more kids. It's shocking and shameful and it needs to stop.

Abuse in Religious Settings

Speaking of churches, NO religion or place of worship is free from child sexual abuse. If you believe it can't happen in your church or synagogue or mosque or temple, you are sadly mistaken. Media stories about abusive priests make it appear the problem lies solely within the Catholic Church (which has documented more than 100,000 victims in the U.S. alone!). But child abuse can flourish in any type of religious organization.

---

xii Remember, research shows that kids are far more likely to be sexually molested or assaulted by straight people. In fact, gay individuals are responsible for less than 1 percent of child sexual molestations and assaults.

And it's such an unfair fight. Religious leaders are held in high esteem and hold positions of power over their flocks, which look up to them for moral guidance and salvation. Religious organizations offer the perfect storm of conditions that nurture abusive leaders, who:

- Operate with little oversight; those organizations that do provide oversight are often willing to overlook immoral behavior
- Have free access to emotionally vulnerable populations of children
- Have the trust of parents—who may not believe their children's allegations
- Often know their congregation members' deepest secrets, which they can use to manipulate or threaten victims
- Are often viewed as God's intermediaries, giving them ultimate power over their victims

No wonder survivors of abuse by religious figures are less likely to report it (nearly 70 percent never tell) than victims of abuse by people in other types of organizations (54 percent of whom don't tell).[50]

Medical Professionals

Larry Nassar, the now infamous doctor for the USA Gymnastics national team, sexually molested and assaulted more than 250 young athletes over 25 years despite numerous reports that were ignored by Olympic and Michigan State University officials. Another case involved Dr. Earl Bradley, a pediatrician, who drugged and assaulted over 1,000 tiny tots, all while videotaping his crimes!

Doctors, nurses, dentists, hygienists, physical therapists, and mental health professionals are people we turn to when we're most vulnerable because we're usually in physical or emotional pain. We *need* them and we trust them with our well-being.

It's so easy, even for adults, to be too intimidated to say anything if these people step over the line. We tell ourselves that we must have misinterpreted what happened or that it's no big deal that our gynecologist touched us inappropriately "down there." Hell, most women aren't even honest with their hairstylist when she screws up, so how do we expect to be able to speak up to a medical professional who's in an even greater position of power?

Again, very few adults and even fewer kids tell anyone when something inappropriate occurs. It doesn't help that when allegations are made, the perps are rarely held to account and the number who actually lose their license to practice is pitifully small.

At least with doctors, dentists, and mental health providers, you can usually find online reviews that will help you learn more about any complaints that have been made against them.

The Federation of State Medical Boards offers a search function at www.DocInfo.org that shows actions taken against a specific physician. You can also conduct an online search for other types of medical professionals by typing in the search box: [his/her name] + complaints + [your state].

Please, please, please never leave your child alone with a medical professional during an exam unless she's old enough to want you out of the room, and even then, always ensure there's a nurse present.

Employers and Coworkers

Having a job not only gives your kid pocket money, but it also gives him a strong work ethic and teaches him skills he'll use for the rest of his career.

But know that teenage workers employed in the hospitality and retail sectors experience the highest rates of sexual harassment and violence on the job. And because they work part-time, they may not receive appropriate training and information about sexual harassment policies, workplace rights, and remedies if they are harassed or assaulted.

On top of that, they're young and inexperienced and likely (unless you've shared with them what you learned in this book) don't have a clue about what's appropriate and what's not, let alone how to stop it.

According to a study entitled Adolescents at Work: Gender Issues and Sexual Harassment, two out of three high school girls and one out of three boys reported being sexually harassed at work, most often by co-workers (61 percent), followed by supervisors (19 percent), and customers (18 percent).[51]

This study and others found that these experiences can seriously harm a survivor's future career path and economic well-being. For example, teenagers who experience workplace sexual harassment are more likely to experience higher levels of stress, academic withdrawal, and school absences, and demonstrate depressive symptoms that lasted nearly 10 years after the incident.

Victims may also struggle with productivity and abandon certain career paths due to harassing behaviors they experienced, or they may accept sexual harassment and violence as a "normal" part of work. As a result, early exposure to workplace sexual harassment disrupts young workers' career paths and overall well-being, leading to poorer health outcomes and diminished economic security.[52]

Ways to Thwart Abuse by Authority Figures

Below are some ways to keep your kid safe from predatory authority figures:

- Educate your kid about what constitutes inappropriate behavior and teach her that it's okay to say no to adults, even doctors and religious leaders.

- Teach your child about the importance of telling you if she's asked to keep secrets from you.

- Get involved. The more present you are in your child's activities, the less access a perp will have to her and the less likely it is that something will happen.

- Closely watch the leader's interactions with her young charges. Watch for grooming behaviors like those I described in Chapter 1 and call them out when you see them. Let the leader know you're paying attention. Strong parental oversight is a HUGE predator repellant!

- Make sure coaches and troop leaders are adhering to the "Rule of 2," which states that there should always be at least two adults present at all times when working with a lone child.

- Never allow coaches or other group leaders or volunteers to be alone with your kid on an overnight trip, such as an athletic competition or band trip.

- Regularly check in with your child and ask what was good and bad about practice. On occasion, ask if anyone makes her feel uncomfortable.

- Be alert to changes in your child's personality or behavior, such as suddenly wanting to drop a club or sport she was enthusiastic about before.

It'll be much harder for a predator to take sexual advantage of your child if she's already aware of predatory grooming behavior. Teach her what appropriate and inappropriate touching and behavior between adults and minors is. Tell her to inform a trustworthy adult *immediately* if her coach or another adult touches her in an uncomfortable way. Let your kid know that it's okay to say no, even to adults.

Badass Grandma's Two Cents

My key takeaways:

1. Nearly 4.5 million K-12 students have experienced inappropriate behavior by a teacher or other school official, including lewd comments, exposure to pornography, peeping, and grabbing. And three million students have experienced sexual touching or full-on assault.

2. Ninety percent of youth organizations don't conduct any type of criminal records check on volunteers and almost half don't even check their references.

3. Educate your kid about what constitutes inappropriate behavior and teach her that it's okay to say no to adults, even doctors and religious leaders.

It's easier and more comfortable to believe our leaders are totally trust-worthy and safe, but you and your kid need to remain vigilant around *anyone* they're interacting with who's in a position of power over them.

Help your kid set and know how to maintain strong boundaries, and teach him to trust his feelings when someone makes him uncomfortable or afraid and then *take action* by getting away from them AND reporting their behavior.

PART II

Where Danger Lurks

In this section, I go into detail about specific dangers you might worry your tween or teen will encounter. This is pretty deep stuff, but it's important that you become educated about these types of threats, so you know how to protect your kid against them.

Later in the book, I refer often to the chapters in this part, so please be sure to read them through. Hang in there! We're working our way to the solutions.

CHAPTER 6

Bullying and Cyberbullying

Imagine if every morning, as you got ready for work, you knew your boss would bully you. Every night you'd worry about what was in store for you the next day, and every morning you'd dread going to work. You'd feel fearful and anxious; you might even throw up.

Now, what if no one believed you or other people who witnessed your humiliation did nothing to defend you? What if they told you to respond to your boss in kind, which YOU know would only make things worse? What if some of those people, secretly relieved that the boss' attention wasn't on them, started treating you badly too? You'd feel isolated and helpless. And as the abuse relentlessly continued, you'd become depressed, hopeless, and maybe even suicidal.

What would you do? Well, as an adult, you have several options. You could:

- Report the abuse to Human Resources
- Quit and find a new job
- File criminal charges if the abuse turns physical or sexual

Now imagine you're 10 or 14 or 17, and you're dealing with this kind of nightmare every day. As a kid, your options are far more limited. You can't always count on the school to put a stop to it, and you may get a less-than-helpful response from your parents, who might tell you to stand up for yourself or work it out on your own.

This is the reality for millions of kids every day in the U.S.

While researching bullying and cyberbullying, there was SO much information available that it was agonizing work trying to capture all the pertinent details and fit it all into one chapter. I read dozens of books and studies on the topic and found them to be all over the board with their advice.[xiii]

I'm going to cover as much information here as possible, so you'll have an overview of what bullying looks like, who the offenders and victims are, how to help your kid deal with bullies, and the short and long-term consequences of bullying.

A Very Wrong Rite of Passage

I'm guessing that as long as there have been humans on the planet, there have been bullies. In my "Disco Queen" heyday in the late '70s, the worst we had to worry about was being challenged to a fistfight behind the gym. Although every young man had a shotgun on a rack in the back window of his pickup truck (this was Arkansas, mind you), no one ever brought a gun into the school. I never even heard of a knife being used.

Bullying is most simply defined as aggressive behavior that can be verbal or non-verbal, physical, or relational (I'll explain that term in a sec) that targets victims, often based on their perceived weakness, appearance, race, religion, gender, sexuality, or disability. Sometimes, there's no apparent reason someone is chosen as a victim; they may just fall out of the bully's favor.

For too long, bullying has been perceived as a rite of passage that kids have to deal with as a normal part of growing up. But when it involves threats of harm or actual physical assault, bullying is a form of criminal behavior and should be treated as such.

Many people believe bullies are social outsiders who secretly suffer from low self-esteem, anger issues, and poor self-control. Certainly, some bullies

---

xiii There are thousands of excellent books on this subject you can choose to read, some of which I reference in this chapter and on my website. I provide great basic information, but if your child is being bullied, I urge you to read other books devoted to that topic to help guide you.

are like that, but others are popular and confident; if anything, they suffer from an overabundance of self-esteem and an inflated sense of entitlement.

Yes, I Actually Said That Out Loud

I'm gonna take a hit for this, but I'll say it anyway because it's true: kids can be such buttheads sometimes—to their parents, to their siblings, and most of all to each other. Of course, not all kids are schmucks, but almost every child goes through phases—think of puberty or any time you try to get them to put down their electronic devices. They're just... so... grrrr... that you want to pinch their little heads off. You wonder what happened to your sweet, affectionate kid.

Wake up, Momma! Move on, Dad! Those golden days are over. Until they grow a fully formed frontal lobe and get a clue, most tweens and teens have to be survived, much like an 18-year-long bout of COVID.

Surviving the Grade School Gauntlet

- Fact: *Millions* of kids are bullied each school year.
- Fact: 85 percent of the time, no one—not friends, other kids, teachers, or other adults—tries to intervene to stop the bullying.[53]
- Fact: 60 percent of students rate bullying as a major problem affecting their lives.[54]
- Fact: Most fifth through twelfth graders are more concerned about emotional maltreatment and social cruelty from peers than anything else, including academic achievement.[55]

I think it's safe to say that we've got a serious problem on our hands.

What Bullying Looks Like

It's shocking to me that when an adult physically assaults someone, it's a crime, but when kids do it to other kids, it's called "roughhousing."

This is true even at school, and yet schools aren't that great at keeping tabs on what's happening in their halls. For example, in North Carolina,

where I live, 72 percent of the state's K-12 schools reported ZERO bullying incidents to the federal government in the 2015-2016 school year![xiv]
Compare this with the 19 percent of NC students who say they were bullied. This isn't just ludicrous; it's putting our kids at risk.

According to bullying experts Deborah Carpenter and Christopher
J. Ferguson, bullying behavior shouldn't be confused with horseplay,
good-natured teasing, or brief clashes between kids in the halls. "Friendship troubles, squabbles between classmates, and the all-in-good-fun wrestling match that gets a little out of hand are normal; sticking a foot out
to intentionally trip (and possibly hurt and humiliate) a younger child is
not," they state.[56]

Bullies are inventive, and bullying comes in myriad creative forms, from
"direct" bullying (involving face-to-face interactions) to "indirect" or relational bullying (involving emotional, verbal, or social mistreatment that
turns victims into social outcasts).

Boys and girls exert social control differently, which means they bully
differently. Girls generally use relational aggression, while boys are more
often physically aggressive. Girls also tend to control or dominate through
social exclusion—withdrawing friendships, not inviting others to parties,
or giving the silent treatment. Boys tend to be more direct in expressing
anger and get over it more quickly, while girl bullies tend to carry resent-
ment longer.

Let's cover these in greater depth.

Direct or Physical Bullying

Physical aggression gets the most attention from schools, parents, and the
media. It includes physical acts or "in-your-face" threats of harm between
an aggressor and victim.

---

xiv Apparently, school officials don't want to besmirch their perfect "zero
tolerance" records, but I'll bet they'd cry like little bitches if they were ever bullied
themselves.

Deborah Carpenter describes it this way:

"Typically, the behavior is action-oriented, involving such behaviors as hair pulling, pinching, pushing, shoving, slapping, kicking, tripping, poking, stabbing, spitting, hitting, punching, head butting, choking, imitating wrestling holds, throwing an object at someone, pushing books out of one's hands, and hiding or destroying property. Girls are more apt to use mild physical aggression, such as pulling hair, slapping, and scratching; boys are more likely to punch, shove, and throw objects.

"Physical bullying can occur even when there is no actual physical contact. The bully can shake his fist in your face, slam a book down on your desk, or invade your personal space. This is referred to as posturing. Posturing is a common scare tactic bullies use to intimidate and frighten their victims. Once a bully gets a reputation for being violent and cruel, a simple threatening move like a fisted hand or a mock air punch can strike fear into a bullied child's heart. The threat of physical violence is sometimes just as effective as actual physical violence.

"Another form of physical bullying involves actions meant to sexually intimidate or harass. A sexual bully might lift up a girl's skirt, 'pants' a boy, push the bodies of two kids together, pinch someone's bottom, grab a girl's breasts or snap her bra, make unwanted sexual advances, or pressure someone into unwanted sexual activity.

"One of the biggest problems with continuous physical bullying is the potential progression and escalation of violence. If the bully trips or shoves you today, what will he do to top it tomorrow? The danger for ever-increasing levels of violence exists."[57]

Although bullying can happen anywhere, it occurs mainly where there's little or no adult supervision, such as at the bus stop or on the bus and at school in the hallways, bathrooms, lunchrooms, or the quad. It also happens wherever groups of kids gather unsupervised.

Relational Bullying

This type of bullying is insidious and can be even more damaging to a kid's self-esteem than emotional or physical aggression. "Mean" girls, especially, love to use this method to terrorize and demoralize their chosen victims.

In her Popsugar.com article, author Sara Ahmed writes that relational bullying focuses on the victim's discomfort and humiliation for the group's entertainment.[58] This can include excluding the victim from conversations or activities, gossiping about her, highlighting her supposed faults, or spreading false rumors about her that cause her social harm. The hurt is often compounded by the fact that the victim's "friends" will often join in with the bully's tactics in order to fit in and deflect negative attention from themselves.

Ahmed offers a list of examples of relational bullying that make me wince just reading them:

- Excluding a member from their own social group: "We didn't ask you to go to the party because we thought you wouldn't be interested."
- Making friendship conditional: "You can sit with us if you promise not to laugh like a donkey."
- Using negative body language around the victim, e.g., constant eye-rolling or smirking when that child is talking.
- Making fun of the victim's appearance: "You're so ugly... just kidding."
- Discouraging others from being sympathetic to the victim: "Are you in love with him or something? Don't be such a baby; we're just playing around."
- Not allowing the victim to make any type of mistake: "Did you see how she tripped on her own shoelaces? This girl is the shoelace tripper. Remember the time you tripped over your shoelaces?"[59]

Most kids are desperate to fit in and be considered popular. What's so awful about relational bullying is that it can destroy the victim's reputation and social standing for days, weeks, or even years.

Who the Bullies Are

Bullies Who Suffer from Shame

Kids who believe they're unlovable, incompetent, or somehow inadequate often suffer from low self-esteem and even shame. To explain shame, compare it with guilt—guilt is "I did something wrong," whereas shame is "there's something wrong with *me*." Big difference. The latter points to feelings of inadequacy so deep that they make the person feel inherently flawed and loathe themselves.

To compensate, kids who live with shame may bully others to cover their own sensitive feelings or divert attention from their perceived shortcomings.

Bullies Who Are Victims or Witnesses of Violence at Home

Kids who witness or are victims of domestic violence at home often embrace the victim mentality or bully persona themselves. Seeing a parental figure yell at, threaten, or hit others in the family teaches kids that this is how people treat each other.

Some kids may carry that behavior to school and bully their peers because they don't know any other way to relate to them. Others may become bully-victims (described below) who are done with being the victim and morph into bullies to gain a sense of control and power in their very disempowered lives. And some may bully their peers because they'd rather be like the more "powerful" abusers in their lives than the "weaker" victims, having seen the price the victims pay.

Bully-Victims

Bully-victims are kids who have themselves been bullied by peers, siblings, or parents. They're tired of being the one without power, so they flip from being the victim to being the aggressor, targeting the most vulnerable kids to gain a sense of power and control. Their aggressive behavior keeps them at the bottom of the social ladder, which feeds their anger and sense of powerlessness. This is called the bully-victim cycle because it feeds on itself.

Bullies Who Are "Good" Kids

This type of bully is confident and believes he's superior to his peers. He may be a star athlete or sit on the Student Council and feels entitled to lord it over others. He loves to show off his superiority and power by bullying kids he considers weak. He has plenty of friends who encourage his aggression, either because they're bullies too or because they fear becoming his next target if they don't go along with his antics.

Bullies Who Are Sociopaths or Psychopaths

Few people understand the difference between sociopaths and psychopaths. Both suffer from deep psychological issues that cause them to lack empathy for others or feel little to no guilt for their bad actions. Both may superficially appear charming and glib, while on the inside, they care only about getting their own needs met, up to and including the desire to intentionally hurt others.

However, sociopaths may be able to form deep bonds with those they care about, and their anti-social behavior may lessen over time. Psychopaths, on the other hand, feel no remorse for their crimes and care about no one. These people don't bully out of retaliation, to preserve their social standing, or to gain the respect of their peers. They bully "simply because they can," Carpenter writes.[60]

Group Bullies and Toadies

Unlike other types of bullies who act alone, the "good kids" and bully-victims may bully as a group, egging each other on as they pick on their victims. Being part of a crowd led by an alpha male or female encourages the group members to do and say things they likely wouldn't do on their own. The relative anonymity of the group has a disinhibiting effect, which can lead to truly heinous behavior (think gang rapes or group fights targeting a single victim).

Many bullies have "toadies"—other kids who follow them and tacitly or overtly encourage their attacks on others. Often, these groupies side with the bully to avoid becoming his victim.

Girl Bullies

If I asked you to envision the typical school bully, you'd probably picture a boy. But girls are just as likely to be bullies, especially when it comes to dishing out emotional, verbal, and relational punishment. "Sticks and stones may break my bones, but words can never hurt me" is BS. Everyone knows physical wounds can heal, but emotional scars can leave a lasting impact on victims. And girls can be positively *vicious* when it comes to dealing with indirect abuse.

Once they get into middle school, girls begin to rate themselves and each other by who's in their inner circle, how many friends they have, how pretty and cool they are, and how popular they are. It's an *all-out war*, and the prize is popularity and loyalty. To ensure she wins, a girl bully will choose who the losers are and then mercilessly exclude them. Her friends back up her bullying behavior because they don't want her critical eye to fall on them.

Bullies Who Have Learning or Behavior Disorders

Kids with attention deficit/hyperactivity disorders or some type of learning or developmental disability that makes it hard to control their emotions and impulses often have few friends and feel lonely and frustrated by their poor social skills. When stressed, some may fly into a rage and act out by harming or threatening to harm other kids. Their excess energy, poor impulse control, and frustration and embarrassment over their learning difficulties just exacerbate their behavior.

Who the Victims Are

There are two main types of bullying victims—passive children and those considered "provocative."

According to Carpenter, passive victims tend to be anxious, nonaggressive, and physically weaker than their peers, with few or no friends to turn to for protection or support. They may suffer from low self-esteem and are unlikely to try to defend themselves.

Provocative victims are often both anxious and aggressive, with poor impulse control or social skills and a tendency to irritate and alienate others. These victims may have a developmental disability like attention-deficit/hyperactivity disorder or autism that makes them prone to react angrily, and sometimes violently, if taunted.

Bullies love to provoke these kids and then sit back and watch them spin out of control. And because the victims may already have a bad reputation for acting out, teachers are often quick to blame and punish *them*, rather than the offenders, sometimes even when they (the adults) witnessed the bullying that led to the outburst.

Special Classes of Victims

LGBTQIA+

The spectrum of gender and sexuality is amazingly diverse. Sadly, out of ignorance or fear, some people target and victimize LGBTQIA+ individuals. People who identify as lesbian, gay, bisexual, transgender, queer/questioning, intersexual, asexual, or other gender/sexuality identity (nearly 20 percent of Gen Z kids[xv][61]) are at tremendous risk of being bullied and/or assaulted.[62]

Here are some stats to consider:[63]

- Seventy-four percent of LGBTQIA+ students have been verbally bullied (e.g., called names or threatened) because of their sexual orientation) and 55 percent because of their gender expression.

- Thirty-six percent of LGBTQIA+ students were physically bullied (e.g., pushed, shoved) because of their sexual orientation, and 23 percent because of their gender expression.

- Forty-nine percent were cyberbullied.

- Thirty percent of LGBTQIA+ students missed at least one day at school in the past month because they felt unsafe or uncomfortable, and 11 percent missed four or more days in the past month.

---

xv Gen Z kids were born between 1997 and 2012.

Our current social and political climate is increasingly hostile to LGBTQIA+ youth, especially those who are transgender, with some states even passing laws that literally outlaw their identities!

Because sexual identity is one of the most central aspects of a person's personality, it can be devastating and even traumatic to have one's gender identity or sexual preference mocked and punished by others.

It's tragic but unsurprising that the suicide rate for LGBTQIA+ youth is four times higher than for heterosexual youth.[64]

Children with Physical, Learning, and Developmental Disabilities

Children with disabilities are at a greatly increased risk of being bullied due to their physical vulnerabilities and compromised social skills. In extreme cases, for example, those involving bullies who expose children with allergies to the items they're allergic to, it could even result in serious injury or death.

As I mentioned earlier, some kids, due to the type of disability they have, are considered "provocative," meaning their poor social skills and low impulse control tend to alienate their peers. It can also bring out the worst in bullies, who get a kick out of harassing these kids until they lose it. The teacher then punishes the victim, having not witnessed the bullying behavior that prompted the outburst.

If your child has a disability or special health issue, you'll want to ensure her Individualized Education Plan (IEP) includes a solid plan to protect her from bullying. If bullying does occur, it may be considered "disability harassment," which is prohibited by the Americans with Disabilities Act.

In Chapter 12, I'll talk in detail about how to empower and protect kids with disabilities.

Clues That Your Kid Is Being Bullied

Kids can be moody, surly, and uncommunicative on an average day. So how do you differentiate between "normal" anti-social behavior and symptoms that your child is being bullied in some way?

You know your kid better than anyone. Look for behavior that's different or inconsistent with her usual personality and ask questions to determine whether it's a temporary phase or something more serious that needs your attention or intervention.

Deborah Carpenter details several symptoms to watch out for, which are listed below. (Seriously, read Carpenter's book; it's one of the best ones I found on bullying and cyberbullying.)[65]

When kids are victimized in any way, they tend to blame themselves and internalize their feelings. Bullying is incredibly stressful, and when your child's body is under stress, it produces too much of the "fight-or-flight" hormones (adrenaline, norepinephrine, and cortisol), keeping her in an aroused state of hypervigilance that leads to a host of physical and psychological symptoms, including the following:

Physical Symptoms

- Digestive issues, such as constipation or diarrhea
- Fear of using the bathroom at school (where bullies can torment her out of sight of the adults), causing her to run home to use the toilet
- Eating disorders, such as anorexia, bulimia, or bingeing (with or without purging[xvi])
- Nervous tics or habits, such as sudden nail-biting or stuttering
- Changes in body posture or body language
- Torn or soiled clothing (indicators of physical bullying)
- Scratches, bruises, or other injuries
- Frequent stomachaches or headaches
- Refusing to go to school or ride the bus
- Faking illness to get out of going to school
- Sudden or chronically bad grades
- Skipping or dropping out of school

---

xvi Purging = Intentionally making one's self vomit after eating.

- Cutting or hurting herself
- Trying to bring a weapon to school to protect herself

Emotional Symptoms

- Anxiety and nervousness
- Sleep disturbances, such as insomnia or night terrors
- Isolating herself
- Clinging or reverting behavior, such as bedwetting
- Dissociation (being mentally "checked out")
- Unexplained emotional outbursts
- Depression, sadness, lack of interest in activities or hobbies she used to enjoy
- Behaving out of character
- Secretive behavior
- Trouble establishing and maintaining healthy relationships
- Loss of confidence and self-esteem
- Expressions of helplessness and hopelessness
- Negative self-talk
- Seeming happy on the weekends but anxious on Sunday nights or at the end of a holiday when she has to return to school
- Sudden interest in personal safety
- Talking about or attempting suicide

The Consequences of Bullying

Bullying hurts everyone involved; it even hurts our society by making the world more dangerous and threatening.

For the victims of bullying, most physical wounds will fade over time, but the emotional wounds can last a lifetime. Even short periods of emotional or relational abuse can cause a child to harshly blame herself and decide she really is a loser. This loss of self-worth and self-esteem can impair your kid's ability to be successful in school and, later, in her career and relationships.

Kids who internalize their abuser's voice in their head may engage in self-sabotage and develop learned helplessness, meaning they no longer try to make things better because they believe their efforts are futile.

There's a true story about elephants that illustrates this: In the olden days, when a baby elephant was sold to a circus, the owner tied a rope around one foot and the other end around a tree. The baby would try over and over to wander but was always thwarted by the rope. Over the years, the elephant learned the limits of the rope until, eventually, the owner would untie the rope from the tree. The elephant could go as far as he liked now but wouldn't wander beyond the length of the original rope because he'd become so used to that limitation.

That is learned helplessness, and it can affect your child in much the same way. She can essentially give up hope that things will change or get better. She accepts her fate as a victim and enters into a vicious cycle in which she's likely to be further bullied or victimized in other ways.

On the other hand, your child might become hypervigilant, making elaborate plans to avoid the bully to the point that it occupies all her attention. As a result, her school and other personal relationships begin to suffer.

Bullycide

When a child is bullied relentlessly and no one intervenes to protect her, she may not see a way out of the torment and might attempt or actually commit suicide. This has become common enough that there's a term for it: "bullycide." Kids who are bullied are more than twice as likely to attempt suicide as kids who aren't being victimized.[66] (Boys are *seven times* more likely to successfully kill themselves.)[67]

One suicide can create a domino effect, with other kids also living in despair following suit. Kids who've lost a classmate to suicide are five times more likely to attempt suicide, even when they didn't have a personal relationship with them. It's like the first suicide gave them *permission* to end their own suffering. Twelve-to 13-year-old kids are at the highest risk.[68]

If someone at your child's school has committed suicide and your child has talked about suicide or you fear she'll attempt it, I urge you to find a therapist to work with her to deal with her feelings.

Why Kids Don't Tell

Sixty-four percent of kids who are bullied don't report it to their parents or authorities.[69] While you want your child to tell you if she's being bullied, in her mind, she may have good reasons for not telling:

- She's embarrassed to be a victim.
- She doesn't want to worry you.
- She may assume you'll tell her to work it out with the bully, ignore him, or tell her to "toughen up" and move on.
- She's afraid you or others won't believe her or, conversely, that you'll overreact and stop her from communicating with her friends. (This would be a common, knee-jerk reaction that could keep her silent the next time something happens. Better to reward her for showing good judgment and being mature enough to recognize when she's in danger and ask for help.)
- She's afraid you'll try to confront the bully or his parents.
- She's afraid of getting the school authorities or police involved.
- She fears being seen as a narc or tattletale.
- She's afraid of retaliation or becoming even more vulnerable to the bully and others if she tells.
- She's fearful of being blamed, especially if she did or said something to instigate or exacerbate the bullying (by making a mean comment herself, for example).
- And, most disturbing of all, she believes she deserves it.

Why Parents Don't Take Action

Parents also don't always react appropriately when they learn their child's been bullied. They may:

- Feel helpless to do anything themselves and expect their kid to ignore it or handle it on their own
- Not know how to react appropriately and so do nothing

- Believe bullying is a rite of passage that their child has to learn to deal with on her own
- Lack sympathy, as in, "I was bullied, and I survived. So can you."
- Fear making things worse for their kid if they intervene (although, it usually gets worse if they don't)

If your child confided in you that she's being bullied and you reacted badly, you can repair the damage by talking to her and apologizing. Assure her that you'll protect her from now on. Ask how she thinks the two of you should handle the situation. Just remember that YOU are the parent and that you'll most likely need to report the incident(s) to her school and possibly the police.

How to Bully-Proof Your Child

Kids see and understand so much more than what we give them credit for. They know what's up, and unless they're just starting school, they've likely already seen bullies at work. Studies have found that bullying and teasing are among kids' top worries (along with school shootings). Teaching your kid how to deal with bullies will empower her to quickly nip bullying in the bud.

Talk Early and Often

The best time to talk to your kid about bullying is *now*, whether she's being bullied or not. The sooner you start the conversation, the better prepared she'll be to deal with bullying if she encounters it.

Asking your kid if she's witnessed or experienced bullying opens the door for her to come to you if something happens. Talking through scenarios and role-playing her responses will teach her how to react in the moment if she *is* confronted by a bully.

It's important to define for your child what bullying is and is not. Teaching her the difference between occasional teasing (done in good fun), rudeness (done out of thoughtlessness), meanness (done with the intent to wound, but not rising to the level of threatening behavior), and actual bullying can help her put other kids' behavior into perspective.

The first thing to teach your child is that no one deserves to be bullied and that there's nothing she does that causes her to deserve being targeted. *It's not actually about her.* Tell her that bullies act out in order to appear cool and powerful. Because they're insecure, they choose to hurt others to make themselves feel better, or they may be afraid that if they don't join in the bullying, they'll be targeted themselves. It could even be a combination of these.

Bullies want to inflict damage on their victims' confidence and self-esteem and say things that may or may not be true just to get a reaction. Most books about bullying advise kids not to take it personally. Hell, even grown-ass adults take things like that personally, so how can we expect a kid to be more mature than we are?

That's why it's good to talk about this before something happens, so you and your child can discuss it when things are calm and she's not in crisis mode.

If your kid has been or is actively being bullied, assure her that it gets better and show her how to defend herself verbally and physically (if necessary), which I'll talk about shortly.

Encourage Your Kid to Remain True to Herself
The most important thing you can teach your child is to be true to herself, no matter what's happening around her or to her. Here in the U.S., individuality and uniqueness are valued and celebrated. This is a difficult concept for kids to grasp because many of them so desperately want to fit in.

They fear that if there's something about them that makes them stand out, they'll be shunned or even punished by their peers. Wearing glasses, dressing out of fashion, being shy or dorky, being a nerd, having a different sexual orientation, or having some type of disability—anything that makes them appear different—can make them a target.

What makes me saddest about this is that the attributes that make a child a target for bullies are often the very things that make them special and most lovable. Having their peers use those traits against a child can destroy her sense of worthiness and self-esteem in ways that can take years to repair.

If your kid is obviously different from her peers in some way (e.g., super shy, socially awkward, or physically different), you'll need to work extra hard to bolster her confidence and help her appreciate her special contribution to the world. (In Chapter 13, I share ways to increase your child's confidence and self-esteem. Check it out!)

Because the consequences are so great, most kids try to fit in, even if that means contorting themselves into pretzel shapes to do so. But to do this, they have to hide their true selves, and that leads them to become inauthentic. People, especially kids, can easily spot inauthenticity, and it can bring the hammer down on the victims even harder.

What's ironic about this is that nearly all kids feel like dorks and are faking it just as hard as everyone else. Even the bullies are afraid of not fitting in, which is why they act like such a-holes in the first place. By making their victims the focus of everyone's attention, they're hoping to distract others from their own perceived shortcomings.

The fact is, the other kids aren't thinking about your kid much, if at all. They're thinking and worrying about themselves. So, tell your snookums to stop obsessing over what other people think! Encourage her to wear her dorkiness like a badge of honor. Teach her that in the real world, outside of grade school, kindness and generosity are what help people get ahead and find happiness and success.

Remind your kid how adorable puppies with crooked smiles are and how much we treasure rocks, animals, and trees that are different from all the others. Bolster her confidence by telling her that when she's true to herself and acts with authenticity she'll feel and appear cool to others because confidence is as awesome as it gets.

The way to be cool is to glory in not fitting in.

Point out how her idols (e.g., musicians, movie stars, even superheroes) all have flaws and are dorks too; that it's okay, and even better than okay, to be different. Remind her that these people wouldn't be famous if not for their unique qualities. Caution her that not everyone can be popular and about the high cost of popularity (again, inauthenticity). Does she *really* want to be like that?[xvii]

Jennifer Hancock says:

"The great thing about embracing your inner dork is that it takes all the stress off of you [the child]. Once you stop trying to fit in, you can relax and be yourself. So, what if someone calls you a dork? You are – 'nuff said. Teasing simply doesn't work on someone who has embraced the fact they are a dork, and they are different. It also frees you up to really enjoy the things you like. Even if what you really enjoy is classical music and you dream of being an opera singer someday, you don't need to hide that from your friends. Not everyone has those talents or dreams, and it is pretty darned cool if you do. So, embrace that about yourself and pursue the things that truly interest you. The point is, when you accept and embrace whatever it is that makes you different, you inoculate yourself against the bullies because they can't make you feel ashamed of something you aren't ashamed of."[70]

I love that.

But what if your kid has a physical or developmental disability or other attributes (e.g., being smaller, bigger, or poor, for example), which make her more likely to be targeted by bullies? The same rules apply. There are kids out there with these types of challenges who refuse to apologize for who and how they are, and they're more respected as a result.

Of course, being confident and authentic doesn't guarantee your kid won't be bullied, but it might help her not to take it so personally. Combine that with the proactive and defensive tactics I teach next, and she'll be better able to respond to bullies in ways that are more likely to quickly put an end to the taunting.

---

xvii Be prepared for her to say yes to this question. If so, impress upon her that there's always a high cost to fame that few are really ready to pay.

Talk to Your Kid about How to Respond to Bullying

The bullying cycle usually begins with verbal harassment before escalating to more serious behavior. Your kid's reaction to the bully's very first attempt may determine whether she goes from a one-time target to a long-term victim.

The most common advice bullied kids receive from well-meaning parents is to just "ignore it and they'll go away." That's helpful if the bullying is limited to simple name-calling or teasing, but when it involves physical harm or threats of harm, all bets are off.

Just ignoring the bully usually doesn't work. After all, if your child is constantly exposed to this person at school or on the bus, the threat of harm is ever-present. Better to tell your kid not to positively reinforce the bully's behavior, which is very different from simply ignoring it.

Positive reinforcement means reacting in any way that's satisfying to the bully—whether that's crying, cowering, acquiescing, or getting angry. Your child's best course of action is to deny bullies what they're looking for by not giving them the satisfaction they're hoping to get. When your kid reacts like a victim, the bully gains power and may continue to pick on her because he's "rewarded" when he does.

To reiterate, when your child denies the bully that satisfaction, she becomes less interesting as a victim. By denying the bully his emotional reward, your kid will make it less worthwhile for the bully to pick on her. She's basically training the bully to leave her alone.

Teach your child specific things to do and say in response to bullying behavior that will deny the bully his satisfaction. For example:

- Embrace being the butt of the joke. When your kid makes jokes about herself based on what the bully says, it puts her in control of the situation and denies the bully the upset reaction he's looking for.

- Respond with as little emotion as possible. Advise your kid to wear a poker face and not give the bully the satisfaction of an emotional reaction.

- Respond with good humor or positive emotions. Teach your kid to act like she's thrilled that the bully noticed her, agree with the bully, thank the bully for his interesting perspective, act with boredom or disinterest, or respond with the same phrase every time (for example, "Thanks for sharing."). This will suck the oxygen out of the bully's fire and cause him to give up on his quest to get a reaction from your kid.

- Teach your kid to be fearless, to accept that she's being targeted, and to not let it bother her so much. Help her realize that since it isn't about her or what she does or doesn't do, the bully has some measure of power over her. However, she has the power to choose how to react. Tell her to use that power to free herself from worry and fear.

There are a number of other ways your kid could respond to a bully. She could:

- Avoid the bully whenever possible. If she must, she can ask for a different locker to avoid bumping into him in the halls.
- Buddy up with a friend to keep from being alone around the bully.
- Agree with the bully ("You're right, I am a klutz.") and walk away.
- Roll with the taunts. ("You're right, my last name *does* rhyme with 'butt.'") and walk away.
- Make a self-deprecating joke ("You're right, I suck at math!") and walk away.
- Own her personality ("You're totally right, I'm a dork and proud of it!") and walk away.
- Ignore him and walk away.
- Tell the bully to stop in a clear, firm voice AND WALK AWAY.

You may have noticed the repetition in the examples above. Prefacing her responses to the bully with "You're right" shows confidence and takes the wind out of his sails. And walking away after responding puts distance takes her out of the range of fire.

Role-play these responses with her at home, taking turns acting like the bully and the victim until she feels comfortable saying them in a strong, firm voice. Even have her practice walking away while you (pretending to be the bully) try to get her to react. (Just don't take your mock bullying comments too far so you don't end up hurting your child's feelings.)

If she can't walk away from the bully because she's cornered, she can continue using the verbal responses above until (a) the bully gets tired of the game he's clearly not winning, or (b) the bullying escalates into an attack, in which case she has a decision to make about whether to fight back or not.

Let her know that fighting back if she must, to keep from being assaulted, is the last resort. But if she feels it's necessary to protect herself, she can choose to do so. Assure her that the consequences from the school are less important than her safety.

This is important: Know that when your brave child uses these tactics to "train" the bully to leave her alone, the offender might not give up right away and may even escalate his behavior. Teach her to expect this and tough it out until he gives up. The bully may frantically attempt to reassert control, but if your kid continues to deny him a reaction, he'll eventually give up. *But she has to be consistent and not give in!* Giving him what he's looking for will only make the situation worse.

Be sure your child doesn't post the anti-bullying tactics she's employing on social media or share them with other kids, so they don't come to the attention of the bully and lead him to increase the abuse.

Jennifer Hancock warns that "Once you stop responding to bullies the way they want, their obnoxious behavior spikes and becomes more frequent and more severe as they try to get you to respond. This is known as a blowout. If the blowout fails to get the desired response, their attempts will fall off quite rapidly. Eventually, they stop trying altogether. The good news is that the blowout means you are close to extinguishing the behavior. The bad news is that because we are all humans with real human emotions, not broken vending machines, most people give in at this point and respond to the bullying."[71]

If, on the other hand, the bully acts in a way that's positive, by being nice, for example, advise your child to reinforce his behavior by being nice

BULLYING AND CYBERBULLYING

in return. Bullies seek attention and giving him positive attention when he behaves is a great way to retrain him to behave appropriately.

It's just like with an animal you're trying to train—you give negative reinforcement when they disobey and yummy treats when they do something right. If the bully goes through a period of being good, encourage your child to keep reinforcing it. If he reverts to his old bullying tactics, she should go back to reacting with humor, boredom, or disinterest.

"The beauty of doing this," Hancock writes, "is that it puts you (the child) in control. Yes, they are still being mean, but you are the one in control of the situation, not them. In short, you are training your bullies to not be such jerks. That's pretty darned cool when you think about it. The bonus is that you get to be the cool, calm, collected individual who was able to find compassion for the rudest jerks in the school. And that's something to be proud of."[72]

It can take days to months of doing this before the bully stops, depending on how persistent or insecure he is. This is why it's so important to nip bullying in the bud the moment it starts.

When Self-Defense Becomes Necessary

When bullying turns physical, your child may need to defend herself to prevent further harm. Two things are important here:

1. Your child needs to know that if she's in imminent danger of being physically or sexually assaulted and needs to defend herself against an attacker, she should do what she must to protect herself and worry about the consequences later. Her immediate safety is what's important.

2. Your child also needs to know *how* to defend herself properly, so her actions are effective yet don't go to the extreme.

Enroll your kid in self-defense or martial arts classes, which will give her not only defensive skills but confidence. It's important that she take these classes long enough to become proficient. Taking just a class or two won't help her. She needs to continue to practice these new skills for the lessons to become ingrained in her memory and accessible in a moment of crisis.

For those who can't or don't want to take formal lessons, teach them to use my signature "rabid Tasmanian devil" self-defense moves, which I describe in Chapter 14. Unleashing her "inner Taz" is as simple as using her own bodily "weapons" to repel bullies and other predators. The tactics I recommend are easy to remember and use, and they're quite effective. Any kid (or adult for that matter) can quickly learn and apply them.

Cyberbullying

In this section, I'm going to talk about cyberbullying between kids. I'll discuss other online dangers in the next chapter.

Cyberbullying is harassment that takes place online, including through texts, email, instant messaging (IM), chatrooms, and social media sites. It can be either direct (e.g., threats or nasty messages sent by the bully or her followers to the victim) or indirect (e.g., malicious comments or rumors, pictures, and private messages that are spread online).[73]

What makes cyberbullying so insidious is its relative anonymity, which brings out the worst in both kids and adults and causes them to say and do things they'd never do in person or one on one. And most parents don't monitor their children's online activity (because they don't know how, because they don't want their kids to think they don't trust them, or because they're too busy or disinterested), making it even easy for kids to hide what they're doing.

What Cyberbullying Looks Like

About a third of all teenagers who are online have been victims of cyberbullying.[74] They've gotten threatening messages, had false rumors about them spread online, or had embarrassing photos posted without their consent.

There are so many inventive ways to cyberbully someone, according to author Deborah Carpenter, including:[75]

- **Text wars**—Inundating the victim's phone with hundreds of nasty text messages.

- **Flaming**—A contentious or heated exchange between two or more people, usually in an online forum or chat room or through instant messaging. This can escalate into name-calling and other hateful comments, with others chiming in to further intimidate the victim.
- **Denigration**—A lie or vicious rumor meant to malign the victim's character and reputation through email, instant messaging, websites, or social networks. It may involve posting embarrassing photos of the victim to humiliate her.
- **Impersonation**— Kids today are wicked smart, and some know how to hack into your kid's email and social media accounts where they can send ugly messages that appear to come from your child. In extreme cases, a vengeful perp can post the victim's name, phone number, email, or real address on a pedophile or hate group website, putting the victim in harm's way.
- **Trickery**—Pretending to like the victim, only to set him up for humiliation.
- **Outing**—Sharing information meant to remain private, including secrets the victim has shared, such as their sexual orientation or their phone number and address.
- **Exclusion**—Excluding the victim from social activities, friendships, or conversations can be social death for a kid.
- **Exposure**—Posting compromising photos or videos of the victim online where they live into perpetuity and can come back to haunt her later.

Who the Cyberbullies Are

Any kid can become a cyberbully. Hidden behind their phone or computer screens, kids can say and do just about anything with little to no consequences. The digital world levels the playing field to a certain extent and gives every kid a platform they can use for good or evil.

Kids who would never physically bully another child may engage in cyberbullying and not even see it as all that wrong (although they certainly mean it to be hurtful). After all, everyone's doing it, right?

Of all the reasons kids cyberbully others, most do it to enact revenge against another kid who "deserves it," for fun, to be mean or show off to friends, or to embarrass the victim.[76] Some kids who feel they've been a victim of cyberbullying may hit back with their own insults or mean comments, making *them* the bully now.

Group or "proxy" bullying is more likely to happen online than direct bullying. Proxy cyberbullying involves many perpetrators who focus their hateful attention on the victim. Often the victim doesn't know who all the cyberbullies are and may feel like the whole school has turned against him.

Who the Victims Are

Get this—only 7 percent of American parents say they're worried about their child being cyberbullied, while 33 percent of American teenagers have been victims of cyberbullying.[77] Clearly there's a disconnect.

Other studies put the number of cyberbullying victims at 70 percent,[78] with 57 percent reporting they're cyberbullied on a frequent or daily basis.[79] Twenty-one percent of all young people who use technology have gotten mean or threatening emails, and 13 percent say they've had an experience on social media that made they feel nervous about going to school the next day. Nearly half were cyberbullied by someone they considered a friend.[80]

Victims of cyberbullying are pretty much the same as victims of physical bullying; they're socially or emotionally vulnerable, or they're different in a way that the bully finds offensive or threatening. But with cyberbullying, even popular kids may be targeted if they cross (often invisible) social lines—for example, by breaking up with a boy or girl who is a bully, by making the wrong enemies, or by making a tragic mistake like texting a nude photo to their boyfriend that's then used for revenge porn (which I explain in the next chapter on Online Dangers).

Self-Harm Cyberbullying

Also known as "Digital Munchausen's,"[81] self-harm cyberbullying occurs when a person posts negative comments online about himself. Dr. Elizabeth

Englander conducted a study on this subject and found that 9 percent of high school students admitted to posting false cruel comments about themselves in order to gain attention.[82]

Sounds bizarre, but think about it—if you're invisible and on the fringes socially, or you crave attention and drama in your life, making yourself into a victim is a great way to get noticed and acquire sympathy from your peers.

Jesse Weinberger, author of *The Boogeyman Exists; And He's In Your Child's Back Pocket: Internet Safety Tips For Keeping Your Children Safe Online, Smartphone Safety, Social Media Safety, and Gaming Safety,* there's a good chance your child has been a cyberbullying victim, perpetrator, or bystander; and possibly all three.

What to Do When Your Kid Is Being Bullied or Cyberbullied

If you learn your kid is being bullied, the first thing to do is tell him how sorry you are that it happened and promise you'll work to protect him moving forward. Don't get overly emotional or angry, which could make him regret telling you.

Calmly draw him out to get the whole story and decide together how to respond. Your kid may beg you not to get involved or report the bullying. If the bullying is mild and your child isn't overly upset by it, you can teach him ways to handle it on his own, such as those I suggested earlier.

Letting him deal with a minor bullying situation can increase his confidence in his ability to take care of himself. Be sure to keep the lines of communication open and encourage him to tell you if the bullying doesn't stop or things get worse. Watch for signs that things are escalating and be prepared to intervene at any point you feel your kid is endangered.

However, if your child has been injured or has been threatened with injury, or if the bully is mentally unstable, has a weapon, or has threatened to use a weapon, it's imperative that you immediately report it to the school (and even the police, which I'll talk about below).

With your child's help, document everything leading up to the incident(s) and exactly what happened during and afterward. Include attempts your kid made to protect and defend himself. Stick to the facts and try not to get emotional or take an accusatory tone in your document or any interactions with school officials. This can come off as overly hysterical and put the authorities on the defensive instead of in your corner.

Keep a running log of all phone, electronic, and in-person interactions with school authorities and the police, including who was involved in the conversations, when and where they occurred, and what was discussed and promised. You'll need this record when you meet with school authorities or the police.

Clueless kids, especially bullies, often document their bad acts online to show off to their friends and get social media likes. This is to your advantage because their videos, texts, emails, or social media posts provide great evidence you can use to bolster your child's claims.

Also, document any injuries to your child, including taking photos of his injuries over time until they completely heal. Consider recording a video of your child telling what happened and showing his injuries.

Recognize that your precious angel may not be totally innocent in the matter. While he doesn't deserve to be unduly harassed or abused, he may have contributed to the situation through his own mean or inappropriate comments or posts. Own up to those when talking with school or law enforcement officials, while emphasizing the need to stop the situation from escalating.

Don't try to talk to the bully's parents unless you know them well. It probably won't go down the way you expect, meaning the parents will likely defend their child rather than apologize and make her stop. Better to let the school handle it.

Reporting Incidents to the School

When dealing with school officials, you may get a tepid response at first. Ask for a meeting with the principal, your child's teachers, and the guidance counselor to talk through what happened and come up with a solution.

Bring an ally with you—an advocate or close friend who can support you. This will lead the school authorities to behave more respectfully and make them more likely to take action—because there's a witness. Plus, if you meet with them alone, it's their more-authoritative word against yours if there's a disagreement over what was said or promised in those meetings.

If school officials still try to sweep the situation under the rug, maintain your cool and get the school board or police involved. If the school isn't able or willing to protect your child from the bully, you may need to file a complaint with the U.S. Department of Education (more on this below) or consider changing his school or homeschooling him.

Your job is to do whatever it takes to keep your kid from being harmed. If that means getting a bad reputation as "that parent," so be it.

A Word on Zero Tolerance Policies

When I got the call from the middle school saying my oldest son, then 12, had been in a fight, I couldn't believe it. *Sean? My Sean? He wouldn't harm a soul!* I rushed to my son's side and found him holding a bloody cloth to his mouth where his broken tooth had been shoved through his gums.

According to both Sean and the principal, he was walking to class when another boy pushed him from behind to the concrete and he landed on his face, hence the injury. The attack was totally unprovoked and nothing else happened, but both boys were given a week of in-school suspension.

I. Was. *FURIOUS!* My son was the victim of an assault, and he was going to be punished? The principal explained that it was the school's "zero tolerance" policy to punish both children involved in a fight, regardless of who started or finished it. Despite my pleas and threats to take it to the school board, the principal wouldn't budge. In the end, he gave Sean three days of in-school suspension, and the bully was suspended (out of school) for two weeks.

If that happened today, knowing what I know now, I would have pressed criminal charges and fought harder to keep my son from being punished at all. He was the victim of a crime and should never have been treated like a criminal himself.

In an effort to curb bullying and other bad behavior, many schools have adopted similar zero tolerance policies, which hand down severe punishments for rule violations regardless of the circumstances. When bullying is a "he said, she said" matter because there are no witnesses (or witnesses refuse to talk), innocent victims may be punished too, as my son was.

As impressive as it sounds for schools to employ zero tolerance, it's not fair to victims and may discourage them from trying to defend themselves for fear of being suspended or expelled. And it may discourage school officials from reporting incidents because they want to appear to be on top of problems in their schools.

Another tactic schools use is to require both the bully and victim to go through mediation or conflict resolution. First of all, it's *not* a "conflict," which implies both parties are responsible for the problem; it's a victimization, and the victim needs to be protected from the bully and not forced to sit across from her and be responsible for stopping her behavior. The number one priority should be stopping the violence and keeping the victim safe. Your child's school may need you to remind them of that.

Actions that are more effective include graduated sanctions, which provide more appropriate consequences for the bully, as well as counseling and peer mentoring that can modify their behavior.

If your kid has been bullied or tells you it's a problem at his school, talk to the principal about how the school addresses the problem and encourage him or her to implement bullying prevention training and strategies, which are known to reduce bullying by as much as 50 percent.[83]

When to Take It to the Next Level

If your kid has been physically assaulted or received dire threats of harm, you can always take legal action, ranging from obtaining a restraining order to filing a police report to suing the bully's family in civil court.

Deciding whether to report bullying incidents to the police can be a tough call—except when your child has suffered physical harm or threats of harm. In those cases, you *must* get authorities involved before a tragedy occurs.

In any event, if your child's school isn't being responsive and doesn't effectively protect your child, you can file a formal complaint with the U.S.

Department of Education's Office for Civil Rights. Your child is protected by Title IX, which is a federal civil rights law that prohibits discrimination in any K-12 school, online school, college, or university that receives federal funding. Title IX provides protections and remedies for victims of gender-based harassment, bullying, sexual harassment,[xviii] dating abuse or intimate partner violence, and stalking.

When your child is granted protection under Title IX, he may be eligible to receive accommodations, such as having the bully moved to a different classroom. (I go into detail about Title IX in my handout on Legal Remedies, which can be found on my website's Freebies page.)

Badass Grandma's Two Cents

My key takeaways:

1. When kids are victimized in any way, they tend to blame themselves and internalize their feelings. Bullying is incredibly stressful, and when your child's body is under stress, it produces too much of the "fight-or-flight" hormones, keeping him in an aroused state of hypervigilance that leads to a host of physical and psychological symptoms.

2. The bullying cycle usually begins with verbal harassment before escalating to more serious behavior. Your kid's reaction to the bully's very first attempt may determine whether she goes from a one-time target to a long-term victim.

As long as humans have walked the earth, there have been bullies among them. It's an intractable problem with no easy solution. But you, as the parent, can help your child better navigate this reality by arming him with the tools and tactics I laid out in this chapter.

And, even more importantly, raise your kid to be a kind, considerate human being who knows not to treat others badly, and help him develop solid personal boundaries she can rely on to protect himself.

---

xviii "Gender-based" harassment or bullying occurs when a student doesn't conform to gender stereotypes (e.g., targeting a person because of their gender or sexual identity, or because they don't act the way a boy or girl "should").

CHAPTER 7

Online Dangers

I chose to create a separate chapter about online dangers so we could look beyond cyberbullying into the even darker world of online child sexual exploitation. The internet is arguably the greatest invention of all time. It's brought the global community together in amazing ways, but it's also made us—and especially our kids—more vulnerable to bad people who want to take advantage of them.

While most other types of crime are decreasing, online sexual exploitation of children is increasing at an alarming rate. Already one of the biggest and fastest growing crimes, online child abuse and exploitation spiked as the pandemic forced kids indoors and had them spending more time on the internet.[84]

According to the National Center for Missing & Exploited Children (NCMEC), since the COVID-19 pandemic began, reports of online enticement of kids have nearly doubled! In 2020 alone, more than 21.7 million reports of suspected child sexual exploitation were made to NCMEC's CyberTipline, the highest number ever received in one year.[85]

The online world is one area where teaching your child to be wary of *all* strangers is a good thing. More on that later. First, let's make sure we're clear on what's what.

More Scary Stats to Make You Take This Seriously

I'm gonna throw some more scary stats out now and follow it by adding a bit of perspective:

- The average teen spends almost 11 hours per day consuming online in content (print, TV, radio, web, etc.).[86]
- Thirty-eight percent of teens have received sexually suggestive content through an electronic device.[87]
- About 40 percent of kids have *sent* sexually suggestive content on-line.[88]
- More than 38 percent of teens say they've had sexually suggestive text messages or e-mails that were originally meant for someone else, shared with them.[89]
- Twenty percent of kids 12 to 14 who engaged in sexting were more likely to engage in oral sex and full-on intercourse than kids who didn't.[90] *(Holy moly!)*
- Young children are becoming addicted to online pornography, with their first exposure occurring as young as the age of eight.[91]
- Half of the victims of online sexual exploitation are between the ages of 12 and 15.[92]
- Nearly 90 percent of all sexual advances toward children take place in internet chat rooms and through instant messaging.
- In 82 percent of online sex crimes against minors, the offender used the victim's social networking sites to gain information about the victim's likes and dislikes,[93] and 65 percent used these sites to gain home and school information about the victim.[94]
- Sixty-three percent of teens said they know how to hide what they do online from their parents.[95] (Think you know what your kid is doing online? Guess again!)

A Few Definitions

Online Child Sexual Exploitation includes:

- The production, possession, downloading, and distribution of child sexual abuse and exploitation materials online
- Grooming children for sexual purposes

- Sexting

- Sextortion

- Online child sexual abuse and exploitation happening in real-time

Social Media: Websites and apps that enable users to create and share content or to participate in social networking.

Chat rooms: Online spaces where users communicate with one another through text-based messages (It's like a virtual cocktail party, where strangers gather to flirt, argue about politics and sports, ask for advice, talk about shared hobbies and interests, or simply hang out.)[96]

Cybersex: Engaging in online sex-oriented conversations and materials.

Sexting: Sending sexually explicit messages or images via electronic devices.

Trolling: Antagonizing others online by deliberately posting inflammatory, disruptive, or offensive comments or content.

Cyberstalking: Using electronic communication to harass or threaten someone with harm.

Sextortion: Extorting money or sexual favors from someone by threatening to reveal evidence of their sexual activity.

Dumbphone: A mobile phone that allows calls and texts, but doesn't access the internet.

Smartphone: A mobile device that's linked to the internet, text messaging services, and apps that provide access to every ugly bit of information on the web. It also provides potentially dangerous people a way to communicate with—and even groom—your kid.

The World Wide Web Is the Wild, Wild West

When your kid goes online—through his computer, laptop, tablet, e-reader, smartphone, Apple iTouch, or gaming console—he instantly has access to every piece of information that can be found on the world wide web (unless you've smartly put monitoring software on those devices).

And it's free, free, FREE! Or at least it doesn't cost *money*. Never forget that if you're not paying for a product, you (and your kid) *ARE* the product!

I simply don't have room in this book to go into great detail about the pros and cons of the various devices or the types of vulnerabilities these create, so if you're interested in diving deeply into these topics, I highly recommend you read Jesse Weinberger's excellent book.[97] It's a super informative and highly entertaining read.

Are YOU Ready for Your Kid to Be Online?

Before you ever let your child touch any electronic device that connects to the internet, you need to be sure that YOU'RE ready. What do I mean by that? I mean that when you accept your solemn responsibility as a parent teach you kid what's okay and not okay online, you must be willing to set meaningful boundaries that are backed up by real consequences. You'll need to supervise his online activities and regularly monitor his conversations and provide corrective advice to keep him within bounds.

If he goes beyond those boundaries and breaks the rules you set, you must then be willing to be the bad cop and dish out appropriate punishment and consequences, up to an including smashing his phone or computer. Yes, I said *smash,* and I meant it. I'll talk more about when this is warranted below.

When to Give Your Kid a Smartphone

So how do you determine the right time to let your child have his first mobile phone? Your kid and the smartphone makers won't like it, but the longer you wait, the better off he'll be.

The general consensus is that kids are ready for their own mobile device (not necessarily their first *smartphone* yet) sometime between the ages of 12 and 14, depending on their level of emotional maturity. Later is better because smartphones can be addictive distractions that detract from schoolwork while exposing kids to issues like online bullies, predators, and sexting.

"The longer you keep Pandora's box shut, the better off you are," asserts Weinberger, an internet safety speaker who gives presentations to parents, schools, and law enforcement officials. "There's no connection to the dark side without the device."

Let's start with a bit more context. Weinberger surveyed 70,000 children and found that, on average, pornography consumption began when children turned eight, pornography addiction took hold around age 11, and sexting began in the fifth grade.[98]

A great option to buying a standard smartphone, which opens up the entire online world without limits, is to get him a Bark phone that enables you to choose what features your kid has access to. It's fully customizable, allowing you to manage your child's entire digital experience, from approving contact requests to managing screen time during the school day. You can allow more functionality as your kid is ready or even "dumb down" the phone so it only makes calls. It's affordable and, because it's a Samsung phone, it's something your kid won't be embarrassed to carry around.[xix]

Truth is, your kid doesn't *need* a smartphone to live. Deciding when to let your child have the freedom of access to a smartphone provides is a tough call for any parent. They'll beg and plead. They'll assure you that every other kid in school has one. (They do not.) They may even threaten to run away or worse if they don't get a phone, but if you're not ready, do NOT give in.

So, I ask again. Are *you* ready to be the adult in the room and provide your child with the guidance and appropriate consequences he needs to stay out of trouble or, worse, harm?

I hope like hell you said yes because if you said no or waffled because you prefer to be your child's BFF than his parent, then you're putting him at serious risk of being harmed—emotionally, physically, sexually, and/or legally.

If you just "can't" have the online dangers conversation with him, then don't let him have any devices that can access online content or conversations. Otherwise, you're being willfully obtuse.

---

xix   You can use my affiliate link to get a discount on any Bark product at: http://bit.ly/CJScarlet_Bark.

PLEASE step up here. Reading this book is an excellent start to picking up the mantle of authority and doing right by your child.

Is Your Kid Ready?

Have you ever compared today's movies—with their action scenes transitioning so quickly that I, at least, have trouble following them—to those made in the '70s? Or watched your kid text? Her little thumbs fly so fast your eyes can barely detect them!

Your kid's growing brain has developed to ingest a large amount of data in a short span of time. It's a quantum leap from the way things were 25 years ago when you were young, but it's your kid's reality and it's all she's ever known or can even imagine. As Weinberger cleverly wrote, fish don't realize they're surrounded by water because they're so immersed in it. In the same way, kids can't see the difference between the real world and the digital world.[99]

Your child's job is to be a kid, which means testing boundaries, making mistakes, and figuring out who she is. Your job as a parent is to help her do all these things in a safe manner. That means setting firm boundaries that allow her to make and learn from her mistakes, and that encourage her to form her unique identity. Believe it or not, kids actually crave fair and consistent boundaries because it gives them a framework to work within and, yes, something to push against.

You crave them too. It's helpful, is it not, when your boss gives you parameters to work within when you're working on a new project, as well as regular feedback to let you know you're on the right track? It's also helpful to get kind, constructive feedback when you're off base.

It works the same way for kids. They want and need your guidance and even your punishments to help them learn how to navigate the world they live in.

Jeepers Creepers, How the Lingo Has Changed!

Is it just me, or does it seem like our kids speak a different language these days? Every generation has its own lingo its denizens use to sound cool and trendy. Nowadays, when something is awesome, it's "sick," and if you say, "it's the bomb," you're clearly out of touch.

If you really want to know what your kid is saying, look up the phrases she uses on www.urbandictionary.com. Warning! Your hair is likely to turn white and you may experience severe nausea and vertigo when you read some of the definitions. The site is VERY graphic.

Our clever kids have devised a whole new lexicon using acronyms to communicate online and on their phones. The ostensible reason is that SMS only allows a certain number of characters in messages, so people have to keep them super short. Think X, formerly known as Twitter, with its limit of 280 characters.

The real reason, however, is that these acronyms act as a secret code kids use to communicate with one another in a language parents don't understand. For example, did you know that POS stands for "parent over shoulder?" If your child writes POS in a message while you're peeking at their online activity, they're telling the person on the other end to keep it clean and appropriate until you're no longer looking.[xx]

How Online Predators Decide Who to Exploit

Just as in real life, online predators carefully choose their victims with intention, based on signs they're looking for, such as a child's obvious lack of self-esteem or confidence, susceptibility to flattery, and statements she makes that indicate she's lonely and hungry for attention and affection.

Perps also get additional info online by paying attention to "sexy" profile names, images, and posts that are provocative and send the message that the child is open (knowingly or unknowingly) to engage in sexually explicit conversations or in-person meetings.

And just as your kid can lie on her profile and claim to be older, many online perps lie to appear and even sound (using voice-changing technol-

---

[xx] To learn what these acronyms stand for, go to www.netlingo.com for a comprehensive, up-to-date list. As with the Urban Dictionary, be prepared for your eyes to bug out and have a trash can nearby to throw up in.

ogy) closer to the victim's age; so that cute 16-year-old boy could actually be a predatory 50-year-old man.

How Perps Get Access to Your Kid

It's so easy for predators to meet your child online. Often, to gain access to chat rooms and instant messaging platforms, your kid has to fill out a profile where she can inadvertently give out personal information that can entice predators. Below are the most common ways perps meet kids, as described by Brian Cox, author of *Child Safety & Protection: Child Security for Parents & Children:*[100]

- *Chat rooms*: The most popular chat rooms for both children and pedophiles are game rooms, child-oriented sites, and teen sites.
- *Email:* If your child gives out her email address to someone she doesn't know, their communications become private and she can hide their conversations from you simply by saving them in a hidden folder and then deleting them from her email inbox, so, if you look just in her inbox or sent folders, you won't find anything suspicious.
- *Instant Messaging:* IM sites are similar to chat rooms, but the communication is more private and one-on-one. It's also live, so the conversation can quickly escalate into inappropriate comments, suggestions, and requests.
- *Websites:* While websites aren't used for direct communication, your child can run across sites that promote hatred, violence, sexual images, or pornography, many of which ask for personal information that naïve kids often provide.
- *Smartphones:* A whopping 95 percent of teens have access to a smartphone, and 45 percent are online "constantly."[101] Smartphones are kids' favorite way to access all the above because they can do so anywhere, anytime, and out of sight of their parents.

Chat Rooms Are the Devil!

Remember that 90 percent of sexual advances toward kids are made through chat rooms and instant messaging. Chat rooms are so appealing to predators because the conversation can take place in real-time, one-on-one, or with multiple people. It's fun, it's fast, and it's lively. It's not surprising that chat rooms are kids' favorite way to communicate.

Your child can also hide behind her profile, so there's a level of anonymity, which tends to have a disinhibiting effect that encourages people to be more outgoing, candid, vicious, and sexual. This anonymity gives your kid a false sense of security that could lead to real trouble.

That PlayStation Isn't Just a Game

Video gaming systems have changed significantly from the time I bought my sons their first Nintendo in the early '90s. Now they can stream movies and shows and enable players to compete and talk trash with other players across the planet. Fun? Yes! Potentially dangerous? Most certainly.

For example, online predators use the chat feature to meet and groom unsuspecting kids. According to Kaspersky, which provides cybersecurity solutions, while online gaming can provide quality social interaction, there's also a darker side. From cyberbullying to predators to hidden costs, there are many concerns when it comes to playing video games online, especially for kids.

There's even a video chat feature that provides visual access to your child, so the perp can see him. (The video chat feature has the added benefit, for the creepers, of ensuring they're talking to real kids and not undercover cops posing as children to catch predators.)

The most important thing you can do is to establish a dialogue about safe online usage as soon as your kid begins playing video games and build upon that as he gets older. When he understands the risks and the importance of security, he's more likely to come to you with red flags or smaller things that worry him.

You need to protect your kid when he's gaming just as you would when he's on his computer or smartphone. Through the gaming console settings, you can enable parental controls and disable internet access and video streaming features. You can also install parental control software to ensure your kid is fully protected while gaming. Parental monitoring apps will notify you if harmful or inappropriate content is detected.

An interesting and essential exercise would be to play along with your kid or watch him play. Ask him to show you how he uses the chat and video features to communicate with other players. Of course, it's up to you whether you allow him to use those features but know that thar be dragons and use those parental controls!

And for the love of Mike, *please* don't let your kid play games that aren't rated for his age! I know of parents who cave in and let their young kids play mature-rated games like "Grand Theft Auto," where they can kill cops and prostitutes and commit other mind-numbing mayhem. Your child may throw a screaming tantrum when you try to limit his gaming options but let that badass parent flag fly! It's better to have an angry kid than a damaged one.

Pornography

Before the internet existed, a kid's first exposure to porn most likely occurred when he stumbled on his dad's or older brother's stash of dirty magazines. The photos could certainly be shocking to an innocent child seeing a fully nude woman for the first time, but the magazines usually didn't show full-on sex acts.

Fast-forward to the Internet Age and we have a different game on our hands. Online pornography leaves *nothing* to the imagination, and a shocking amount of it features illegal images of children being sexually abused and tortured.

As I wrote earlier, the average age a child is first exposed to porn (by accidentally stumbling upon it online, through friends, or by seeking it out) is around 11, but, as I also noted, some kids as young as eight are regularly consuming pornography online.

A national survey revealed that 84.4 percent of 14-to-18-year-old males and 57 percent of 14-to-18-year-old females have viewed pornography.[102] As you can see, it's not just our sons we need to worry about.

A study performed by BitDefender, an internet security software provider, found that kids under 10 account for 22 percent of porn consumption. The study also found that while 97 percent of parents used parental control software to block access to adult websites, 12 percent of their teenagers succeeded in uninstalling or unlocking this software.[103]

It's not a question of *if* your kid will be exposed to porn, it's a matter of *when*. Role-play with him what he should do and say if someone tries to show him pornography (in a magazine or online). For example, he could say, "I don't want to see that. It's gross," or "I'm not looking at that. My mom/dad would kill me," and then walk away.

Child pornography—now called Child Sexual Abuse Imagery (CSAI) to better reflect what it is—is any depiction of a minor or an individual who appears to be a minor engaged in sexual or sexually related conduct. This includes pictures, videos, and computer-generated images. Even altering an image or video so that it *appears* to be a minor can be considered child pornography.[104]

The FBI's Child Victim Identification Program has received nearly 300 *million* videos and images of child sexual abuse acts since it was launched in 2002. And these images are shared through any of the untold numbers of child porn forums and networks or via live streaming, which show the abuse of children *as it's happening* to an eager paying audience. Because it's streamed in real-time, it's even more difficult for authorities to detect and stop it.

Porn has always been popular with a certain crowd, but the advent of the internet has made pornography instantaneously accessible and even free. It's also made more people perceive viewing porn as a socially acceptable activity.

It is not.

Why Porn Is a Big Deal You Should Care About

Viewing porn has super-serious long-term consequences that should concern you. According to Dr. Carolyn Ross, "Early exposure (by age 14) to pornography and other explicit material may increase the risk of a child becoming a victim of sexual violence or acting out sexually against another child. For some people, habitual use of pornography may prompt a desire for more violent or deviant material, including depictions of rape, torture, or humiliation. If kids seek to act out what they see, they may be more likely to commit sexual assault, rape, or child molestation."[105]

There are two types of pornography you need to be alert to: (1) pornography your child can readily view in magazines or online through his phone, tablet, computer, or gaming console; and (2) pornographic images (photos and videos) of your child that he himself or someone else takes of him.

Porn Your Child May View

To reiterate: Chances are high that, by the age of 11, your child has seen pornographic material. And since 20 percent of all online porn involves sexual images of children, there's also a good chance your child may have seen another child being abused.[106]

Here's the kicker—you can't blame your kid's dodgy friends for exposing him to porn, because 79 percent of the time that exposure *occurs at home.* Yes, *your* home.[107] Makes you want to run out and buy some parental control software, doesn't it? Good! I'll talk about how to do that later.

Your kid could also be shown porn by a predator who's attempting to groom him. Pedophiles like to view porn and online sex acts with their victims to normalize that behavior and try to sexually arouse them. Research shows that those who view child sex acts may be more likely to act out what they see.

Pornographic Images of Your Child

Seeing pornographic images at a tender age is bad enough, but what predators are really interested in is obtaining sexual images of your kid that they can keep for personal use and/or share with or sell to others.

Many of the online sites dedicated to so-called "kiddie porn" encourage or require members to upload their own images of children being sexually exploited. Sickeningly, they trade images like kids used to trade Pokémon cards.

Revenge Porn

Revenge porn occurs when two people break up and one (or both) of the former partners posts sexual images or videos of the other without their consent to enact revenge by embarrassing them, causing them distress, threatening them, or even blackmailing them.

Over half of older child victims know their offenders in person, often as romantic partners. About a third of them are threatened with physical harm and tormented for more than six months. Half didn't disclose the incidents, and few reported them to the police.[108]

Don't forget that when your tween or teen sends sexual images to anyone, including intimate partners, she runs the risk that her former object of adoration will share those images with his friends (as 38 percent do). And it can get much worse if she ends up being charged with a federal child pornography crime because she sent a naked selfie!

Sexting

You have your head in the sand if you think your child is too young to learn about sexting. Kids as young as 11 are doing it, and you want to nip this alarming little practice in the bud.

Get this: 15 percent of teenagers have sent or posted nude or semi-nude images of themselves to someone *they only know online!* What most adults would consider a stupid move is considered by many kids to be a great idea. (Actually, many adults do this too! Way to be great role models, guys.)

Your kid probably carries the means to her own destruction with her 24/7. It's her smartphone, and with it, she can sext with others and send and receive explicit photos and videos all day and all night long. One Texas study warns that "Sexting is the new first base."[109]

Aaaand this is how sextortion begins.

Sextortion

Here's the general pattern: A predator poses as a younger kid or trusted older mentor and grooms a child for as long as it takes to gain her trust. Next, he tests the waters by throwing out a few sexual jokes or comments to see how the child reacts. If she reacts negatively by setting a boundary and telling the offender to stop, he'll likely move on. If she reacts positively or even neutrally, the perp will press on, eventually asking her to send one sexy photo "just for fun."

Once he gets the nude or semi-nude photo, the predator threatens to reveal the photo on social media and/or tell the girl's friends or parents. The child naturally freaks out because she doesn't want to get in trouble and lose her online privileges for life, and she certainly doesn't want to experience the embarrassment and harassment that would surely follow the photo's release.

So, she does whatever the creep asks, sending more—and more explic-it—photos and videos (which can include the victim performing sex acts and could number in the hundreds or thousands!) or agreeing to meet him in person.

The more images she sends, the more the predator asks for, until the child is in so deep and feels so hopeless about finding a way out that she may even consider suicide to stop the harassment, constant anxiety, and fear. In the meantime, the predator is using the photos and videos for his own enjoyment while almost certainly passing them on or selling them to other predators.

According to the FBI, the major risk factor for kids getting "sextorted" for nude photos is not so much related to them getting online and saying or doing something sexual. Rather, their vulnerability is related to how much TIME they're online. That means that the more time they spend on their electronic devices, the more creepy people they're going to run into and the more likely it is they'll be exploited.

Please read that last sentence again. I'll wait.

Russ Tuttle of The Stop Trafficking Project puts it this way: "It's no different than if we go into the grocery store. If I'm in and out and get what

104

I want, I'm good. If I stay there awhile, 'Oh, I don't really need this, but I think I'm going to go down this aisle, maybe...'"[110]

Tuttle continues, "It's no different for our kids. They're on their favorite app, and someone says 'Hey, check this out! You need to see this!' And all of a sudden, they're on another site, or they're in another social media app. Or maybe they're on that gaming system, and they're communicating with someone, and that person says, 'Hey! I want to show you something.'"

I don't know about you, but I buy more when I shop hungry, *just as a kid who's lonely or looking for attention or affection will be more vulnerable to predators the longer they spend time online.*

As a result of sextortion, child victims commonly experience a range of negative outcomes, including hopelessness, fear, anxiety, and depression. The Cyber Tipline reports that about one in three child sextortion targets engaged in self-harm, threatened suicide, or attempted suicide due to their victimization.[111]

That "Innocent" Sexy Photo Could Land Your Angel in the Big House

Did you know that in most states, if your kid is under 18 and sends a sexually explicit photo of himself to his girlfriend, he could be charged with a felony under current child pornography laws? And be sentenced to actual prison? AND be listed as a registered sex offender for the rest of his life?

Hell, if your kid just reposts or forwards even a sexually *suggestive* photo or video that someone sent him, he could also be charged with felony possession and trafficking of child pornography. This is *serious* shit, people.

This information really shocks and scares me because it could happen to any child, even those with the most vigilant parents. And if you consider that 20 percent of kids admit to having sent genital pics to other people,[112] we could fill our detention centers with child "offenders."

I totally get why the laws are so tough; it's imperative that the government do something to try to curb the sexual exploitation of minors, and there are plenty of victims among that 20 percent, but not ALL of those who post or trade revealing photos of themselves are perpetrators. They're just kids being stupid kids. Yet no matter how much the parties involved protest that they were willing participants, your child could still be charged with the creation and trafficking of child pornography.

And once those photos or videos are "out there" in cyberspace, there's no getting them back. They're online forever. Any potential college admissions agent or employer could (and probably will) look over your child's social media profiles and see shots of her partying like it's 1999 or posing for a nude selfie. Plus, potential employers will very likely do a criminal background check, and you certainly don't want them to find a conviction on your child's record or see that he's on the sex offender registry.

Did I scare the pants off you? Good. You MUST teach your kid not to send or trade sexual images with anyone. *Ever.*

Now, let's talk about how to keep your child out of trouble online.

Laying Down the Law

Great! You've decided to parent up and you're ready to have a candid conversation with your kid about digital dos and don'ts. If he's already happily surfing in cyberspace, start having that conversation at once to ensure he knows what the new rules are (or reinforce the existing rules—that's a gold star for you!).

Below I share with you some of the most important rules you should enforce to keep your child safe. Know, however, that your kid may look you dead in the eye and lie his ass off when you ask him the questions I suggest here. For every social media account and log-in detail he shares, he's likely hiding two more he knows you wouldn't approve of. Just know that going in.

If You Have a Hard Time Saying No to Your Child

If you're worried about saying no to your kid—because you don't know how to set consistent boundaries, because you were terrorized as a child by your parents, because you grew up with no rules at all, or because you're afraid that if you bring the hammer down your kid won't like or love you anymore—this section is for you.

Over the course of his lifetime, your kid will be told no thousands of times—by you, by teachers, by bosses, by friends, and by romantic partners... you get my drift. The sooner he learns to deal with the no's in his life, the better off he'll be. And the bonus is, if you start teaching him when he's young, he'll have your guidance and love to cushion the blows and setbacks along the way. Kids who aren't told no don't develop strong coping skills and have a cosmic bitch slap in store for them when they enter the real world.

When a kid gets his way all the time, the yes's become meaningless and lose their value. It's a bit like having candy with every meal. The pleasure begins to wear off after a while and the sugar high loses its appeal. Although he'll almost certainly protest when you say no, he won't stop loving you and he'll get over it faster than you think.

Kids are so resilient and adaptive. When you put up a boundary in one direction, they'll usually find a more creative, more constructive way to have fun than the one you denied them. Trust that your budding entrepreneur will find a way to act within the boundaries you set and have fun in the process.

With great power comes great responsibility. This is true in all areas of life, and the word "responsibility" needs to be ever-present in your child's mind. Trust me on this, you can't know everything he does online. If you think you can, you're wrong. Your best bet to keep him safe is by ensuring he knows the truth about what goes on online and how to navigate that busy jungle filled with devious and determined predators.

One of the best ways to keep him in line is to allow him to access his (or the family's) computer or laptop *only* in the living room or den, or wherever your family hangs out the most. Your presence and the constant traffic will serve as a deterrent. It'll drive him crazy, but he'll get over it. Also, require that he ask permission first to use the computer.

And if you're really smart, and I know you are, you'll make him earn his screen time by doing chores and/or homework first. (This *really* works!)

What to Teach Your Kid Before He Goes Online

• Install Bark's parental monitoring software to every device your kid can access (family or personal laptops, phones, tablets, gaming systems), and tell him it's there to protect him. This will also put him on notice that his online activity is being monitored. Also get him a Bark smartphone that has parental controls already baked in.

• Learn which apps and social sites are bad news by visiting www.FamilyEducation.com.

• Together, choose the social sites he'll join. Research the pros and cons of each site you consider and select the ones you both agree on. Remember, you're the parent here, and you have the final word!

• Set limits on what your kid is allowed to do online, what sites he can visit, what kinds of content he can post, who he can "friend" and chat with, and what chat rooms he can visit.

• Help him learn how to choose strong passwords. You can create acronyms that have a special meaning to him, like the first letters of the names of his favorite movies or songs, with some special characters thrown in.

• Tell him not to trust anyone—and I mean N-E-1—with his username and password, not even his best friends or siblings. The only person he can share his passwords with is you, his parent. This *must* be mandatory. Inform him that his best friend today could be his worst enemy tomorrow, and that so-called friend could access his social accounts and wreak havoc.

• Help him select an appropriate photo and write a profile that isn't provocative to predators.

• Talk about how predators lie on their profiles and communications and talk about what grooming behavior looks like. Warn him that perps may try to manipulate him by giving him compliments and gifts—a well-known and effective tactic to get your kid to feel like he should give the predator something he wants in return.

- Remind your kid that the photos he posts have location information embedded in the files. This can lead perps to other info that can identify where the child goes to school, who his friends are, etc.

- Tell him not to "friend" anyone online that he doesn't know in real life.

- Advise him to cover or turn off his webcam when he's not using it. People can hack into the webcam and watch your child get undressed, pop his pimples, sleep, etc.

- Ask him what he thinks "sexy" means. Talk about what kinds of photos and videos are considered inappropriate.

- Make sure your kid knows the legal consequences of sexting, which I spelled out above. Even when the photo he sends or receives isn't nude (remember, it just has to be *suggestive*) and even if he didn't take the photo himself, he can still be held responsible. Be blunt about the fact that he can be arrested, charged, convicted, and imprisoned for a federal felony if he sends so much as one nude selfie to his girlfriend. (I'm being a bit dramatic here, but the feds have successfully prosecuted kids as young as 10! They're not messing around, and neither should you or your kid.)

- Tell him that sexting will be interpreted by predators to mean he's willing to have sex with an adult.

- Talk about how sexting can lead to sextortion. Be 100 percent clear that sending a sexy photo to someone online could end up all over the web on his friends' social media and make him vulnerable to sextortion.

- Make it clear to your kid that he must tell you *immediately* if a stranger asks to meet him. This is SO important! Warn him that he should never meet someone in person he only knows online if you're not also present. In addition to thinking they know every damn thing under the sun, kids tend to think they're invulnerable and don't believe they could ever be duped or abducted into a sex trafficking ring, for example.

- Show him how to block, flag, and report abusive content. This is the most effective way to stop bullying behavior. If you don't know how to do these things, research the answer and teach him what you learn so he can handle bullying incidents quickly and neatly.

- Encourage your child to tell you if another kid is being sexually exploited or bullied online so you can let that child's parents know. Explain that seeing and not reporting these crimes makes him guilty of wrongdoing and may make him legally liable, depending on the nature of the exploitation. Encourage him to be part of the solution, not the problem.

- Tell him not to retaliate if he's provoked by someone online, or he may also be guilty of criminal behavior himself.

- Teach your child to trust his intuition; if something doesn't feel right, it's not, and he needs to stop all communication with that person.

- Teach your kid to check in with the "internal parent" in his head before disobeying one of your rules, accessing a chat room or site that you wouldn't approve of, or entering into or continuing a conversation that involves sexual content. Advise him to ask himself: "Will my parents or grandparents be upset or disappointed if I do this?"

- Emphasize that his online reputation is one of his most important assets, one that needs to be closely guarded. Photos of him partying or that contain sexual content will live on the web forever and could ruin his future prospects.

- Reinforce how much you respect him and how much he should respect himself. Teach him that how he behaves online reflects how he expects to be treated by others.

Your kid's computer, tablet, and phone time should be limited to a set amount per day, at your discretion, and be *completely* off-limits overnight. At bedtime, make him turn them over to you to keep in your room every single night.[xxi]

---

xxi My friend once confiscated her 15-year-old stepdaughter's phone and it pinged at 1:30 in the morning with sexts from her boyfriend, shattering her parents' naïve image of her as an innocent angel, which led to a necessary conversation that should have taken place much sooner.

Yes, he'll whine and complain, he might even cry and pitch a fit, but stick to your guns, Mom and Dad! Whether he believes it or not, you're doing him a favor. The earlier you implement this rule, the quicker he'll get used to the idea as just a fact of life.

Questions You Need to Ask Your Kid Who's Already Online

- What social media accounts do you have, and what are your passwords?
- What are your user IDs for each account?
- What photos are you using for your profile picture?
- Have you ever posted something and then immediately or later regretted it? What did you do about it? What would you do differently now that you know better?

Should You (Gasp!) Spy on Your Child?

My short answer to this question is *not exactly*. Rather than obsessively spying on your kid, I advise you to set up strong parental monitoring controls (using apps like those mentioned in the section below) which will automagically notify you of inappropriate activity (e.g., cyberbullying, sexting, talk of suicidal ideation, etc.) so you can take corrective action.

Your precious gosling isn't as innocent as you might like to think. Yes, most kids are genuinely great human beings, but they're still kids and kids across the board do stupid shit. It's part of their learning experience. Remember, good judgment comes from experience and experience comes from *bad judgment*. It's their job to experiment and make mistakes.

So, don't be afraid to monitor your kid's online activity, if only to save her from herself. And let your kid *know* she's being watched; it'll keep her on her toes. Be aware that she'll very likely try to create profiles you don't know about, which is why monitoring software is a must-have. She won't like it but stand firm!

Software That May Protect Your Kid from Cyber Dangers

Below is a brief list of software programs that monitor your child's online and mobile phone activities. Most offer free version with limited features. You'll pay more for premium features, but they're WELL worth the cost! If any of these are no longer in service, there are dozens of great products available, so I encourage you to do your homework to find the best ones. This list is from www.tech-vise.com:[113]

- Bark.us protects and monitors your child's phone, tablet, and computer on over 30 social media sites. It's the bestselling parental monitoring app on the market. Bark also offers a state-of-the-art Samsung mobile device that has robust parental controls and enables you to decide what features your kid has access to (e.g., texting, camera, apps).

  Note: I serve as a brand ambassador for Bark because, after extensive research, I've found their app and mobile device to have THE best features and offer the greatest protections, including covering the most social media apps. They also do the best job of engaging with their customers.

  Bark also offer a kids' smartphone that makes it super easy to protect your child. You can use my Bark affiliate link here to get the best deal.

  (For those who are reading this in paperback form, you can use the QR code I provide at the end of the book to get the best deal on Bark's products.)

- Qustodio.com monitors social activity, calls, text messages, apps, searches, and browsing. It also keeps tabs on picture uploads, screen time usage, and location tracking. Your kid can even activate a panic button for alerts. You (the parent) are in full control of setting up limits and can access these records for 30 days.

- Kaspersky's Safe Kids app tracks your child's whereabouts and device habits, restricts content, balances screen time, and more in their all-in-one app.

- ScreenRetriever enables you to monitor your child's computer activity live wherever the computer is located in the home. You can actually see who your child is communicating with using his webcam.
- Mobicip.com is software that allows you to monitor activity, filter search settings, block content, and even view app use.
- Nischint.com lets you monitor your child's cell phone and online activities. You can also see who your kids talk to on social media and what kind of apps he's downloading. You can also view his SMS and phone logs and track his location.

This Isn't a "Turn the Other Cheek" Moment; It's an "Eye for an Eye" Moment

Rather than simply punishing your kid when he breaks an unspoken rule, which will feel grossly unfair to him and likely spark a rebellion, it's far better to lay out clear rules and the consequences for breaking them in advance and then stick to them.

To help avert "But I didn't know that was wrong!" complaints, type up your ground rules and add a statement promising that he won't disobey your rules or suffer the consequences. Make him sign that contract and keep it handy so you can whip it out when you need to.[xxii]

Of course, you can't foresee every scenario, and you'll have to wing it sometimes, but you can predict a lot of what might happen (because you read this book!). Remember, if you install monitoring apps or software, you'll be able to detect when he's accessed something you wouldn't approve of, and you'll have time to come up with an appropriate punishment.

If your kid breaks a rule you hadn't anticipated, take the time you need to figure out a reasonable punishment and then hand down your verdict. Stick to your guns when you deliver the news. Your child will squeal like a wounded piglet when you tell him you're taking away his phone. He'll beg and plead and promise it will never happen again. He'll yell that you

---

xxii Feel free to use any of the ideas from this chapter in the contract.

didn't have a rule in place and that it's not fair that he's being punished for something he didn't know was prohibited. He may even threaten to harm himself or run away if you impose your punishment.

I urge you, dear parent, to *stand your ground*. He'll eventually get tired and head upstairs or get hungry and come downstairs. Either way, the onslaught will end… for now. After that, he may not speak to you for a while, and his glares may jab a knife into your heart, but you have GOT to stick with your ruling. Otherwise, you're teaching him that the cost of doing what he wants is to make you suffer. You're the only loser in that scenario.

Ensure the Punishment Fits the Crime

But the punishment has to fit the crime; you don't want to smash your kid's phone because he went to a forbidden website. In that case, you might instead calmly reinforce the rule and then suspend his online privileges for a week or two, depending on the type of site he went to. Save the big guns for when he deviates from the rules in a big way that exposes him or has already exposed him to real danger.

At the risk of repeating myself, please, I beg of you, invest in a Bark smartphone for your kid. This Samsung phone is the only one for kids that has tamper-proof parental controls built in and is customizable so you can enable or disable features according to your kid's behavior. So if they show good judgment you can enable more features, or turn off texting or the camera if they abuse their privileges. You can also track your kid's location and even remotely lock the phone, if necessary.

Here are some examples of punishments, just to give you an idea of what's possible. Of course, you alone can decide what constitutes an appropriate punishment for your child; just make sure you've told your kid what these consequences will be *in advance*, if possible.

- For posting private information, like his real name, address, or phone number, make him close down the respective account(s). Watch him actually do this and don't let him open new accounts for at least a month. Take away his electronic devices for a week.

- If he shares his password with anyone other than you and your partner, make him close the respective account and don't let him create a new profile on that site for at least a month. Take away his electronic devices for at least a week.

- If he cyberbullies or encourages the cyberbullying of another, take away all his digital devices (that includes his phone, tablet, computer, laptop, and gaming system) for at least a month. Make him apologize, in person if possible, and make amends to the victim. Make him read one of the bullying books you'll find on the Resources tab of my website (that are appropriate for his age and developmental level) AND write a short report on what he learned to prove he actually read and absorbed it.[xxiii]

- If he includes sexual images or content in his profile name, handle, or avatar, have him close down the respective accounts and don't let him open new accounts for at least a month or more, and only with you standing over his shoulder as he chooses new ones. Also confiscate all his digital devices for a couple of weeks. Then, talk with him about the dangers I cover in this chapter AND write a report on what he learned.

- If he receives sexual content (communications or images/videos), take a screenshot, document the communications that led up to that moment, and call law enforcement. Put a two-week embargo on all electronic devices to put some time and space between your child and the lure of cyberspace.

- If you find out your kid sent sexual content of any kind (including sexts, or sexual images or videos) to another person, you're on Defcon 1! Take away ALL his devices, including his phone, for at least a month or more. After your electronics boycott has ended, either buy him a dumbphone that can't access the internet, or, better yet, get that Bark smartphone that enables him to still make calls, but not send or receive text messages.

---

xxiii I really like this idea of having kids do research to learn why their actions were dangerous and to have to write a report to prove they understood what they learned. It's both informative and suitably painful. You can use this with kids as young as eight.

Yes, you *could* smash his smartphone if you like, just to bring the point home, but you can avoid that expense by just getting the Bark phone and disabling all but the call feature. Let him know he can earn back more features as he shows better judgment and is more responsible over time.

Again, talk with him about the dangers I cover in this chapter and have him write a report on what he learned.

- If you learn that your kid plans to or actually met someone he only knows online, it's time to launch the big guns. This is *very* serious behavior that could leave your child vulnerable to sexual predators or traffickers. In this case, he loses all breathing and electronic device privileges for at LEAST a month and his smartphone for at least two months.

Okay, so maybe don't take away his breathing privileges, but hit him where it hurts (not literally, of course; no corporal punishment, please!). By removing access to his favorite things or activities, even if that means he can't go to the prom or play in the big game, you'll leave a lasting impression that will discourage him from doing that sort of thing again.

Ban him from tagging photos on social media sites or sharing his GPS location (which tell perps where he is). Make him write that report (seriously, do it!) so he knows what kind of trouble this could lead to. When you feel he's learned his lesson, give him back the Bark phone with everything but the call function disabled, or get him a flip phone that can't access the internet.

Now—*as in TODAY*—before anything happens, put monitoring software on all of your kid's electronic devices. Also include any family devices he may have access to. That way, you'll be instantly and automatically notified if something inappropriate goes down.

What to Do if Your Kid Is Being Exploited Online

Be on the lookout for signs your child is being exploited online (e.g., engaging in inappropriate conversations, sexting, being sextorted, etc.). For example, you daughter may suddenly avoid going online or answering her phone, become secretive and try to hide her online activity by changing what's on the screen when you enter her room, or quickly delete messages when you walk by. She may also try to erase her screen history or other files.

As with any of the dangers I talk about in this book, whether your kid comes to you or you learn another way that she's being exploited online, you have to work to appear calm, even if you're totally freaking out on the inside. Do NOT overreact by screaming, sobbing, blaming, or shaming your child, or by threatening to do severe bodily harm to the offender. This will only make her feel awful and possibly keep her from being completely honest with you about all that happened for fear of making you even more upset.

Her biggest fear is that you'll take away her phone or computer privileges—a real possibility—but refrain from immediately taking her devices away until you get to the bottom of the story. Remember, if she came to you for help, you need to take into consideration that (a) it took a lot of courage for her to do so, and (b) she's showing a large measure of responsibility and good judgment by telling you at all. Oh, and (c) she's *talking to you,* which beats the alternative (her silence or a suicide attempt) by a long shot.

Document What Happened

As I wrote in the last chapter on bullying, it's important to keep a log of every interaction your child has had with an offender, as well as all interactions with school (if the offender is another student) or law enforcement officials, so you'll have something concrete to show if you decide to press charges.

Here are some other things you can do:

- Tell your kid to ignore but not delete hurtful or inappropriate comments (so you can maintain a record in the event the harassment escalates).
- Save and print out copies of all online communications to provide a record for schools, police, lawsuits, etc.
- Encourage your child to ID the offender. If a crime has been committed and you know who's responsible, that information will jump-start

any law enforcement investigation. If you don't know who that person is, leave it to the police to investigate; don't play private eye and possibly escalate things or compromise the investigation.

- Clearly and firmly send a message to the online offender to cease and desist his harassment, sextortion, or sexually inappropriate behavior. Tell him you've reported him to the police and that they're investigating the incident(s). Immediately change your child's email and other profiles and block the bully. Ban your kid from visiting sites where the offenses occurred.

- Report the offender to the phone company, internet service provider, AND owner of the website in question. The sexual exploitation of people of any age is against most digital companies' policies and can be prosecuted.

- If the offenses are being committed by another student, report them to the offender's school. Additionally, if the behavior is severe or threatening, report it to the police right away.

- If your kid has been the victim of sexual exploitation, in addition to reporting it to the police, you can file a report online to the National Center for Missing & Exploited Children's CyberTipline at www.cybertipline.com.

Badass Grandma's Two Cents

I just can't stress enough that if you're concerned about digital dangers, you need to read Jesse Weinberger's book *The Boogeyman Exists And He's In Your Child's Back Pocket: Internet Safety Tips for Keeping Your Children Safe Online, Smartphone Safety, Social Media Safety, and Gaming Safety*. It's the most informative and interesting book I've read on online safety. It's also real and realistic and a fast read. It definitely gets the Badass Grandma's Seal of Approval!

CHAPTER 8

Sexual Molestation and Assault

I saw the horrified look on my 13-year-old son's face from all the way across the Olympic-sized pool and knew something was wrong. As I made a furious beeline around the perimeter of the pool, the middle-aged man who was swimming next to him scrambled out of the water and sprinted off in the opposite direction.

For a second, I was torn. Do I chase down the man and tackle him without knowing what had happened, or do I rush to my son to ensure he was okay? I chose to go to my son, pointing madly and screaming all the way, "Stop that man!" As I reached my son's side, I looked up and saw the man run out of the front door and disappear. *Dammit!*

My son was shaken but okay. The scumbag had sidled beside him in the pool and tried to fondle him beneath the water.

I wanted to weep with frustration and sorrow; I had tried so hard to break the cycle of abuse I'd experienced, but I still couldn't keep my son safe, even when he was just a pool's-width away from me.

Yes, I had worked hard on *me*, but I had neglected to teach my kids how to protect themselves when I couldn't. My son didn't know how to react when the man approached him, and he didn't know he could say no to an adult. I felt like a total failure as a parent.

Definitions

Before I launch into the topics of sexual molestation and assault (rape), I'd like to clarify some legal definitions.

Child Sexual Abuse—According to StopItNow.org, child sexual abuse includes "all sexual touching between an adult and a child, and sexual touching between children when there's a significant age difference (usually three or more years) between them, or if the children are very different developmentally or size-wise."

I would add that it includes any sexual contact where one of the participants has not given consent—in other words, they're not okay with what's happening or they're unable to provide real consent because they're impaired by a mental disability or by drugs or alcohol.

StopItNow.org continues, "Sexual abuse doesn't necessarily involve penetration, force, pain, or even touching. If an adult engages in any sexual behavior (looking, showing, or touching) with a child to meet the offender's interest or sexual needs, it's considered sexual abuse. This includes the manufacture, distribution, and viewing of child pornography (now called child sexual abuse material).

"Sexual abuse also includes, among other things, having a child pose, undress, or perform in a sexual manner; spying on a child in her bedroom or bathroom; having a child look at or watch sexual acts in person, in movies, or in magazines; and having noneducational, sexually explicit conversations with a child."[114]

Abusive Non-Touching Acts—Abusive "non-touching" acts include showing sexually suggestive images or porn to a child, talking to her in sexually explicit or suggestive ways via phone, internet, text, or in person; taking sexually explicit or provocative photos or videos of a child; viewing or violating private behaviors such as bathing or dressing; exposing oneself to a child in a lewd way, or making the child expose herself.

Sexual Assault/Rape—Sexual assault can range from unwanted touching and molestation all the way to full-blown rape. It's defined by *Merriam-*

Webster as illegal sexual contact that usually (but not always) involves force upon a person without their consent or is inflicted upon a person who's incapable of giving consent (because of age, physical or mental incapacity, or impairment) or which places the assailant (such as a doctor or priest) in a position of trust or authority.

Sodomy—This term refers to oral and anal sex acts of any kind.

Incest—Child sexual abuse is considered incest when the perpetrator is a biologically or nonbiologically related person who's functioning in the role of a family member.

Online-Mediated Sex Crimes—Sex crimes against kids that are facilitated through online means include the possession, distribution, or production of child pornography; sexual solicitations (online interactions with minors for sexual purposes, including plans to meet offline); and conspiracy crimes such as collaborating with others to distribute or produce child pornography, or sexually solicit or traffic minors.[115]

When It Really Counts, Everyone's Counting Differently

Estimates of the number of children who are victims of child sexual abuse are impossible to pin down because so many kids never tell an adult they've been victimized. They may have been threatened by the perps, or they may be so filled with shame that they fear being blamed for the incidents.

When I researched the statistics on this, they were all over the place. Every time I looked at government agency or nonprofit advocacy sites, the stats were so divergent that it was confusing and frustrating. Some of them even contradicted their own statistics in the same document!

What I *can* tell you from my professional experience in the criminal justice field is that the number of child sexual victims is appallingly high. In my 33 years working with survivors, virtually every single woman and a surprisingly high number of men I've spoken to about this subject have shared that they were either molested or raped, almost all of them as children or young adults. Of these, only a handful ever reported the crimes.

And, of the ones who said they *did* report it, I can remember only *two* that ended up with the offenders being arrested, tried, and convicted.

Who the Perps Are

If you read Chapter 1 about predators, you already know that perpetrators can be found in every shape, size, color, gender, age, socioeconomic level, religious institution, educational background, group, club, sports program, school, college, and university. They can be family members, friends, neighbors, teachers, coaches, religious leaders, or (less likely) strangers.

Here's what we know about the perpetrators:

- Family members are responsible for about a third of child sexual abuse cases.

- The younger the victim, the more likely it is the offender is another juvenile[116] who may be older or bigger, making it a criminal offense. Since nearly 40 percent of abusers are kids themselves, it's important our children recognize that forcing sexual activities on other people is a crime, regardless of the age or sex of the offender.

- Boys make up 93 percent of juvenile offenders.[117]

- Seventy percent of child sex offenders have between one and nine victims, while 20 percent have 10 to 40 victims.[118]

Who the Victims Are

No child is immune from the possibility of being sexually abused. I don't care how nice his neighborhood is or how much money his parents make. I don't even care how hypervigilant his Tiger Mom is; every kid is at risk. That's the bad news.

The good news is that because you're reading this book, you're learning how to protect your kid *and* are empowering him to protect himself when you're not around. By educating him about the dangers the world presents and teaching him how to thwart predators, you're doing the very best you can possibly do for him.

Risk Factors

One thing researchers and agencies *do* agree on is the risk factors that make kids vulnerable to sexual abuse. Please remember that just because a kid has some or even all of these risk factors doesn't make it his fault if he's victimized. It's *always* the perpetrator's fault for choosing to commit the crime. It also doesn't mean your kid *will* be abused; it just means he's more vulnerable to predators because of these factors.

Here we go:

- Children living in foster care are 10 times more likely to be sexually abused than children who live with their birth parents.[119]
- Both genders are the most vulnerable between the ages of seven and 13.[120]
- Boys younger than 12 are three times more likely to be abused than older boys.[121]
- African American children are nearly twice as likely to be abused than white children.[122]
- Children in low-income households are three times more likely to be sexually abused, and those in rural areas are twice as likely to be abused as those who live elsewhere.[123]
- Kids who've witnessed or have been the victim of other crimes are significantly more likely to be sexually abused.[124]

These are just the factors that have been measured. Below are more risk factors that increase a child's risk for abuse. If he:

- Has low self-esteem and lacks confidence in himself
- Is lonely and craves attention and affection
- Has been physically or sexually abused before[125]
- Is also the victim of physical or emotional abuse
- Has special needs, such as a physical or intellectual disability, chronic illness, or mental health issues[126]
- Has parents or siblings with drug, alcohol, or mental health issues[127]

- Hasn't been taught the basics of human sexuality, so he doesn't know what constitutes healthy and unhealthy touching and behavior
- Spends unsupervised time with others, at or away from home
- Is exposed to or has easy access to pornographic images (which he does if he's online)
- Has siblings or parents who've been sexually abused in the past, *whether or not it was ever talked about*[xxiv]

Please pay attention to these. If your kid has any of the risk factors above, I urge you to read Part IV of this book to learn how to teach your child to develop a stronger sense of confidence and self-esteem, set and maintain solid boundaries, develop and act on his intuition, and protect and defend himself so he doesn't become one of the statistics.

A Quick Word about Party Rape

Since we're talking about tweens and teens here, I want to address the topic of party rape.

Seventy-five percent of all acquaintance rapes involve alcohol and/or drugs, and researchers have found that alcohol-facilitated rape is the most common form of sexual violence against women.[128]

Perpetrators who drink prior to an assault are more likely to believe that alcohol increases their sex drive: and are also more likely to think that when a woman is drinking, it sends the signal that she's interested in sex.

Drinking or taking drugs is NOT an invitation to be raped. However, girls are more vulnerable to being raped if they've been doing these things:

---

xxiv Kids are so intuitive and can pick up on the most subtle cues, so even if they haven't been explicitly told that a parent or sibling was abused, it's like they can be influenced by that energy, and it makes them more likely to be abused too.

Speaking of drugs, it's not only the ones your kid voluntarily ingests that you need to worry about. Predators, particularly while in college, may use Rohypnol ("roofies") or dozens of other date rape drugs that can't be seen, smelled, or tasted to incapacitate their victims. Common side effects include drowsiness, amnesia, impaired judgment, and a loss of coordination that can last for hours. These drugs are hard to detect through blood tests once they've worn off, making it difficult to prove the victim was drugged.

Signs and Symptoms of Abuse

Kids can be tricky to read; some are open books and express every emotion they feel, while others are more reserved by nature. When a child has been sexually abused, the experience is often very traumatic and he may even dissociate and become numb, showing no emotion at all.

Still, there are some signs you should watch for that *may* indicate your kid has been or is being sexually abused. You'll note that these symptoms are almost exactly the same as those for bullying and other types of abuse. *Trauma is trauma, and it leaves clues.*

Again, just because your kid displays some or even many of these symptoms doesn't necessarily mean he's been victimized; it may just be normal kid behavior as he transitions to adolescence. But if your child is displaying any of the symptoms below, you need to get to the bottom of whatever's causing his distress.

Even if your kid stubbornly refuses to share with you, I promise you— and I know this from personal experience—he's hoping you'll find out and stop the abuse.

By being observant and keeping the lines of communication open with your child, you increase the likelihood that any incidents will be identified quickly. Better yet, keep reading and I'll show you how to teach your child to set and maintain such strong boundaries that he can stop predators in their tracks *before* anything bad happens.

Back to the signs and symptoms of abuse. I'll jump right in with the big ones:

- Pregnancy (for girls only, obviously)

- Being diagnosed with a sexually transmitted disease or infection (like herpes, syphilis, gonorrhea, vaginal infection, etc.)
- Urinary tract infections, or abnormal vaginal or penile discharge
- Genital or rectal pain or bleeding
- Underwear or sheets that are stained with blood or other discharge
- Pain while urinating or with bowel movements
- Obvious difficulty walking or sitting
- Fearful behavior, such as nightmares or new fears of certain people, places, or things
- Depression or social withdrawal
- Extreme increase or decrease in appetite, or the development of an eating disorder
- Sudden lack of self-esteem or confidence
- Sudden personality changes (e.g., a normally outgoing kid stops speaking, a well-behaved kid develops discipline problems)
- Frequent stomachaches or headaches with no medical cause
- Bullying others or being bullied
- Extremely aggressive or passive behavior
- Overly affectionate or clingy behavior
- Sudden interest in sex or sexualized behavior that seems inappropriate for his age, including excessive touching of his own private body parts, persistent sex play with friends, toys, pets, or other kids, or making drawings with sexual content
- Sexual promiscuity
- A drop in school performance
- Secretive behavior
- Attempts to run away or skip school
- Self-harm of any kind (e.g., cutting, burning, or otherwise injuring one's self, or careless behaviors resulting in self-harm)

The Consequences

Below are some of the short- and long-term consequences your child may experience if she's been or is being sexually abused. Keep in mind that not all survivors are traumatized or negatively affected by the incident(s); it depends on the length and severity of the abuse and the child's ability to cope and adapt. Also, know that many of the problems may not manifest until your child is older. It's not uncommon for puberty to be a trigger.

Compared to her peers, when a child has a history of childhood sexual abuse, she's:

- Far more likely to develop post-traumatic stress, which can lead to abnormal development, dysfunction, and distress well into adulthood[129]
- More likely to engage in high-risk behaviors, such as risky sex or drinking and using drugs. Her likelihood of abusing drugs or alcohol is three to four times higher than for people who were never abused[130]
- More likely to get pregnant as a teenager. In fact, two-thirds of pregnant teens have a history of sexual abuse, and boys who've been sexually abused are more likely to get a girl pregnant[131]
- Nearly 25 percent more likely to drop out of school[132]
- Twice as likely to be arrested for a violent crime[133]
- Twice as likely to attempt suicide and three times as likely to develop a psychiatric disorder[134]
- At greater risk of developing serious health conditions, such as diabetes, cancer, stroke, and heart problems[135]

Talking to Your Kid about Sexual Assault

It's important to talk to you tween or teen about topics like safety and sexual assault. To get them to open up, consider the following conversation starters, provided by RAINN,[136] the Rape, Abuse & Incest National Network:

- **Use the media to make it relevant.** Ask your child's opinion on something happening on social media, in the news, in a new movie, or on a popular TV show. You could even watch an episode with her and ask follow-up questions. Asking her opinion shows her that you value her point of view, and opens up the door for more conversation.

- **Use your own experience to tell a safety story.** Sharing your own experiences can make these conversations relevant and feel more real for teens. If you don't have an experience you feel comfortable sharing, you can tell a story about someone you know.

- **Talk about sexual assault directly.** For most tweens and teens, issues like sexual assault aren't on their radar. On the other hand, they may have misconceptions about sexual assault that they've picked up from peers or the media. Bring up relevant statistics, such as the fact that eight out of 10 instances of sexual assault are committed by someone known to the victim. Explain that no one "looks like a rapist," and that she needs to check in with her gut and trust it when it tells her someone isn't trustworthy.

Badass Grandma's Two Cents

On the Freebies page of my website at www.cjscarlet.com, I provide an article entitled *If Your Child Has Been Sexually Abused,* which offers more information about what to do if your child discloses sexual abuse of any kind. There, you'll also find an article on *Navigating the Criminal Justice Process,* which can guide you in the event charges are filed against the abuser.

It's important that you know that being victimized doesn't mean your kid is doomed to a terrible life. With therapy and a strong support system, many, if not most, survivors—even those who struggle for some time through the healing process—go on to be successful and happy.

Because I didn't seek help for my post-traumatic stress until I was in my 30s, it took years of therapy to work through the trauma. But once I did, I was on fire, and I never looked back! My life today is so sweet and peaceful and filled with joy and gratitude that I can hardly believe it myself. There is a light at the end of the trauma tunnel!

CHAPTER 9

Sex Trafficking

When I was 18, I was befriended by a woman who choreographed the dance routines of a play I performed in. Cindy, an artist, was in her early 30s and when she asked me to model for her and her mother, I was flattered and agreed. (To be perfectly honest, I really did it to freak out my mom.)

As I sat in various stages of undress before the two women, we chatted amiably about our hopes and dreams. I shared my burning desire to leave the small Arkansas town I felt trapped in and of my dreams of traveling the world, meeting fascinating people, and having exotic adventures.

Shortly after my 19th birthday, Cindy called and asked if I was serious about leaving Arkansas. When I said yes, she told me she had good news and to come to her house right away. When I got to the rural home she shared with her parents, Cindy sat me down on her bed and informed me that a wealthy man in Florida had seen one of her paintings of me and wanted me to be his mistress. My stomach began to clench, and I could hear distant alarm bells ringing in my head.

Cindy told me that with my new lover, I would—you guessed it—travel the world, meet fascinating people, and have exotic adventures. The man would also pay for me to go to college, and (here's the kicker), if I was a good mistress, the man would marry me and take care of me for the rest of my life.

I had no idea how to respond. By that time, my intuition was screaming at me to get the hell out of there. But before I could react, Cindy's father walked into the room, and she left. He told me he would drive me to meet this mysterious sugar daddy and provide the "training" required for me to be a proper mistress. Then he attempted to sodomize me.

Somehow, I found the courage to leap from the bed and run outside to my car, slamming down the lock just as he grabbed the handle. As I tore out of the driveway, gravel flying behind me, I heard him yell, "Don't you DARE tell!"

And for years I didn't tell a soul. It was a decade later before it occurred to me that there was no wealthy man waiting for me. With dawning horror, I realized the more likely plan was to get me to Florida under the control of some pimp who would force me into using drugs and walking the streets as a prostitute.

It was another decade before I heard the term "human trafficking," but I recognized it immediately. I also realized, after sharing this experience with a high school friend, that Cindy and her parents had done this to other young women. Cindy has since moved and her father died, but I wonder to this day how many girls were trafficked because I didn't tell.

The World's Fastest-Growing Crime

Sadly, my experience isn't unique. Sex trafficking is the world's fastest-growing crime.[137] In the U.S. alone, hundreds of thousands of kids are at risk for sexual exploitation at any given time,[138] mainly those who are runaways, throwaways (unwanted by their caregivers), have a history of sexual abuse, or have other vulnerabilities, which I cover below.

In countries where poverty is rampant, some parents sell—yes, sell—their children to people who promise to give them jobs but who are actually traffickers. (Before you judge those parents too harshly, try to appreciate that they may sell their children because they believe the lies of the traffickers, who tell them their kids will have a chance at a better life and will be able to send money home to help support the family.)

Children are often targeted by traffickers because they're easier to manipulate than adults and can earn more money over the course of their captivity.[139] Predators carefully groom victims and then use lies, threats of harm, and violence to coerce them into sexual slavery or labor. Some also use professed love for their victims to convince them that prostituting themselves will help the predator and victim financially.

Stats

With child sex trafficking, as with child sexual abuse, the statistics are a bit wonky. I found stats that claim nearly 300,000 U.S. children are lured into the sex trade each year,[140] which includes voluntary "prostitution" (hint: it's not "prostitution"; it's child sexual assault) and may not count as sex trafficking. Other sites I found cite only a few thousand *reported* cases a year.[141] Because sex trafficking victims rarely report their experiences, any estimates are likely grossly inaccurate.

Here are some other statistics to consider:

- The average time it takes for a child to be groomed online is eight days. *EIGHT days.* That's how long it takes for a perp to convince a kid to either meet him or her in person, begin to share nude photos with them, or fall into some other level of sexual exploitation.[142]
- Kids are particularly vulnerable to sexual slavery and exploitation and make up 27 percent of the victims.[143]
- Girls are twice as likely as boys to be trafficked for sex.[144]
- According to the website DoSomething.org, the average age of kids lured into the sex trade in the United States is *12 to 14 years old.* (Read that again.)
- A history of sexual abuse makes children more vulnerable to sexual exploitation. More than 90 percent of kids who are victims of sex trafficking have been sexually abused in the past.[145]
- The largest group of at-risk kids in the U.S. are runaways, throw-aways, or homeless who use sex to acquire food, shelter, clothing, and other things needed to survive on the streets. [146]
- The more stable and functional a home a child grows up in and the more they're protected from any type of abuse or exploitation, the *less likely* it is they'll be lured into a sex trafficking situation.[147]

Who the Perps Are

Before I talk about the characteristics of predatory traffickers, I want to acknowledge the role of the sleazy men and women who actually pay for and are on the receiving end of child sex trafficking. Studies have shown that the majority of these people know full well that the children they're paying for are being exploited... *and they don't care.*[148]

These people are despicable and should be placed on an international sex offender registry at the very least. Few, however, are ever arrested, and those who are usually get only a light slap on the wrist.

The traffickers who supply children to these sick people are master manipulators and employ a raft of tactics that help create a "trauma bond" with their victims. Similar to Stockholm syndrome, traumatic bonding occurs as the result of ongoing cycles of abuse in which the intermittent reinforcement of reward and punishment creates powerful emotional bonds between the victim and her captor.[149]

This bond, along with the constant threat of physical, emotional, and sexual abuse that comes with it, keeps victims trapped and under the traffickers' control. They have absolutely no compassion for their victims or compunction about forcing them into sexual slavery.

Sex traffickers also come from every walk of life. They're professional groomers, always on the prowl for new victims; it's how they make their living, and they live large because of it. (Some pimps earn tens of thousands of dollars each week, allowing the victims who "earned" that money to keep little to none of it.)

Traffickers may work alone or in small groups, sometimes with the help of other young victims who've been forced or manipulated into recruiting new innocents from among their own school or area. Other sex rings involve huge criminal networks that exploit large numbers of victims and are rife with corruption and money laundering.

While some traffickers use brute force to ensnare victims in the sex trade, many find it more effective to use charm (ick). So-called "lover boys" recruit girls as young as middle-school age, showering them with attention, affection, endearments, gifts, money, trips, protection, and promises of a dream life.[xxv]

Brad Riley, the founder and president of iEmpathize, a nonprofit that combats crimes against children, identifies five "disguises" a trafficker may take on to gain his victim's trust:[150]

1. **Pretender**—Someone who pretends to be something s/he is not, such as a boyfriend, a big sister, a father, etc.

2. **Provider**— Someone who offers to take care of an individual's needs, such as clothing, food, or a place to live, or their wants, like cool cell phones, purses, parties, etc.

3. **Promiser**— Someone who promises access to appealing things, like an amazing job, a glamorous lifestyle, travel, etc.

4. **Protector**—Someone who uses physical power or intimidation to control and "protect" the victim.

5. **Punisher**— Someone who uses violence and threats to control the victim. When the previous disguises have been exhausted, an exploitative person often becomes a punisher to maintain control.

Like other predators, these types of traffickers carefully groom their chosen victims, learning what they like and need and then using that information to manipulate them into doing what they want. Once the traffickers secure the victims' loyalty, they convince or coerce them into prostitution, often forcing them to become addicted to drugs to ensure their dependence on them.

Traffickers groom their victims until they're under their full control—through some form of abuse or threats, through drug dependency, by controlling the victims' access to money, by isolating them from their family and friends, or by dehumanizing them through tactics like branding or

---

xxv Ever see one of those bold-faced ads in the classified section of the newspaper promising high pay, monster perks, and, of course, FUN! for motivated candidates? Chances are good that ad is a front for sex traffickers seeking potential victims.

renaming them. At this point, traffickers can force their victims to do any-thing they command.

The victims are, in every sense of the word, their slaves.

Who the Child Sex Trafficking Victims Are

Victims of human trafficking are of every race, social class, sexual orientation, immigration status, and income level. Women and children are the most vulnerable, as are people who have little education, live in poverty, come from marginalized populations, are dependent on drugs, or who grew up in abusive homes. Runaways, especially, are at tremendous risk of being trafficked.

Even kids from loving families with parents who are vigilant about their safety can fall prey to the wily tactics used by sex traffickers. In fact, a sur-prisingly large number of sex trafficking victims continue to live at home with their unsuspecting families while being forced to perform sex acts on the side by their handlers.

Risk Factors

When trolling for victims, traffickers target the most vulnerable kids who:

- Are young (pre-teen and adolescent girls are more susceptible to the manipulations of predatory traffickers)
- Are victims or witnesses of neglect, domestic violence, child abuse, molestation, or sexual assault
- Are victims of war, conflict, or natural disaster
- Are victims of social discrimination because of their race, sexual ori-entation, illegal status, or economic insecurity
- Are runaways, throwaways, and homeless youth
- Have a history of time spent in foster care or juvenile detention
- Are failing in school
- Are into experimenting with drugs or risky sexual behavior
- Are addicted to drugs or alcohol or have a parent with an addiction
- Suffer from low self-esteem and self-worth

- Are desperate for attention and affection
- Identify as LGBTQIA+ and have been kicked out, stigmatized, or rejected by their families

How to Spot a Trafficking Victim

There are signs that *may* indicate a child is vulnerable to being trafficked or is already being sold for sex. Just spotting one or two of these signs may not mean anything, but if they add up, it could point to something significant.

Pay attention when:[151]

- You hear stories about a child under 18 who's said to perform commercial sex acts.
- She has unusual and unexplained sex paraphernalia (e.g., bulk condoms or lubrication).
- She's seen at strip clubs or featured in pornography or, as in my case, is asked to pose nude for an artist or photographer.
- She's featured in online ads, chat services, escort or dating services, or porn sites.
- She works excessively long or unusual hours.
- Her appearance and behavior change and become more sexualized.
- She runs away and is gone for more than 24 hours.
- There are unexplained absences from school.
- She appears fearful, anxious, depressed, overly submissive or shows signs of physical or sexual abuse.
- She suddenly distances herself from her family and friends.
- She has multiple social media accounts that she closely guards and refuses to let you look at.
- She's meeting with new friends she met on the internet.
- She's often seen with a male or female peer or older person who seems to monitor her movements and conversations and may even speak for her when she's questioned.

- She hooks up with an older boyfriend or woman who's abusive or controlling.
- It appears she works and lives in the same location.
- She talks about new job opportunities (e.g., modeling, singing, or magazine sales).
- She suddenly has plenty of money with no obvious source of income.
- She develops a drug or alcohol addiction.
- She develops a sexually transmitted disease, infection, chronic illness, or psychiatric disorder.
- You notice a new tattoo, brand, or burn mark with a strange name that she's unwilling to explain.
- Her behavior changes suddenly and significantly, such as dropping her old friends and hanging out with a totally new crowd.
- She starts using trafficking slang, such as "trick," "the life," or "the game."[152]
- She starts carrying multiple cell phones or other devices.
- There's evidence she's been or will be traveling, or she's living out of a suitcase, car, or motel.
- She resists offers of help to get her out of her situation.

How Traffickers Choose Their Victims

There are several reasons predators choose particular victims, and there are also patterns they look for in their targets' behavior that provide clues your child can use to avoid them. The most essential thing a predator must do to groom his victim is to establish her trust in him.

According to CyberSafeWomen.org, "Predators look first for children who lack self-confidence; who need someone to listen to and understand them; to flatter them; or to reassure them that they're special, attractive, smart, or cool. Predators work to learn their targets' likes and dislikes, habits, and fears, and they pretend to share these. They may buy their victims gifts and shower them with praise, all to convince them they're special and loved.

"They also cater to their targets' need for approval and recognition, to the point that their victims may become emotionally or psychologically dependent on them, making it even easier to manipulate them. With time, the victim becomes dependent on her 'handlers' and may allow the abuse to continue because she's dependent on him for his financial support, or fears she'll be harmed or killed if she leaves."[153]

Ways to Spot a Trafficker

The old adage is true: If something looks too good to be true, it probably is. Teach your kid to pay heed to her intuition in situations where she's approached by someone who promises a better life. Trust me, there's a catch. If she's not sure whether to trust a person who offers her a quick, easy way to make money or to leave her mundane existence behind, help her do her homework.

Conduct a background check on the person and see what comes up. Know that he or she may be using a false name, so an internet search or background check may not provide much information. Your child can also "interview" the person making the offer (with you over her shoulder on a Zoom call) to see how he reacts to your child's questions. Is he evasive when she asks for more details about the opportunity? Does he tell her to just "trust" him without answering her questions? Does he try to minimize her concerns? Does he try to isolate her or turn her against her friends and family? Is he possessive, or verbally, physically, or sexually abusive in any way?

Teach your kid to immediately remove herself from this situation. I'm serious; end all contact and report that person to the police. Her report may stop the creep from luring other unsuspecting kids into sexual slavery.

Getting Help if Your Child Is Being Trafficked

The absolute best way to keep your child from becoming a victim of sex trafficking is to provide her with a safe, loving environment, talk to her in an age-appropriate way about how to protect herself from predators, and keep the lines of communication open.

If you suspect your child is being groomed or recruited by a trafficker, document what you know and share it with the police right away. If you're *certain* your child is being trafficked, just call the police and let them help you document what you know.

You should also call any of the national and international human trafficking agencies I list in the Resources section of my website. These organizations can provide information and connect you to other agencies that can help you.

The Long-Term Consequences

Sexual abuse can have devastating short- and long-term effects for any child, but when your child has been the victim of sex trafficking, the consequences can impact her for a lifetime if she doesn't get help.

Children who've been trafficked, especially if they "loved" their pimp, might not fully understand that what happened to them is considered abuse. And they may feel ashamed because of what they suffered or because they believe they were somehow responsible. If they were separated from their families, friends, communities, or cultures, younger children, especially, may feel alienated and have a tough time reacclimating.

Other consequences may include:

- Pregnancy
- Sexually transmitted diseases or infections
- Ongoing pelvic pain, rectal trauma, or urinary problems
- Psychological problems or disorders
- Fear of intimacy or being alone
- Generalized fear and anxiety
- Depression
- Sleep disorders or nightmares
- Eating disorders
- Drug or alcohol addiction
- Other post-traumatic stress symptoms

Getting Counseling for Your Kid

I cannot stress strongly enough how imperative it is that you get your kid into counseling if she's been victimized in any way. It may be very difficult for your child to talk about her trafficking experience and to trust a therapist, but make her go anyway; it could make all the difference in her ability to heal from the trauma.

Badass Grandma's Two Cents

I was one of the near-victims who came from a loving (but lax) home. I wasn't taught anything about trusting my intuition, setting and defending personal boundaries, or sex in general; PLUS I suffered from PTSD from my earlier abusive experiences, all of which made me an ideal target for the people who attempted to traffic me.

PLEASE continue reading to learn how to protect your child from such a fate. You may think they won't listen, but I assure you they will. And what you teach them could save them from immense trauma and potentially save their lives!

PART III

What Your Kid Needs to Know

A Note About This Section

We want our kids to be safe, so we teach them to wear a helmet when bike riding and to look both ways before crossing the street. But very few parents teach their kids about body safety and consent, or they wait until they think their kids are "old enough" when it may be too late. In my case, my parents NEVER talked to me about body safety or sex, even after I got pregnant at 15.

I'll put myself on the spot and admit, with tremendous regret, that although I had a VERY thorough sex talk with my boys and bought them condoms even before they started dating, I didn't teach them a single thing about how to protect themselves from predators because I didn't know how to do it for myself at that point.

If you haven't been talking to your kid about body safety and consent—because you don't know how or what to say, because you're too embarrassed, or you're afraid of frightening him—don't feel bad; you can correct that right now.

In this section, I first talk about the humongous hot pink elephant in the room—sexual consent, which, if taught properly, can keep your child from ever becoming a victim or inadvertent (or advertent) perpetrator.

Next, I break down the most important things to teach your child, and I promise you it's not as hard or embarrassing as you think. I've included an entire chapter just for parents of kids with disabilities who are even more vulnerable to predators, so you know how to talk to them at their developmental level.

Obviously, I couldn't cover every single scenario in this section. To learn more about any given topic, I encourage you to refer to the resources I offer on my website.

Before I dive into these topics, I first want to talk about your kid's brain.

Your Child's Brain Isn't Fully Cooked Yet

If you ever took Psych 101, you've heard of Maslow's Hierarchy of Needs. For those who haven't, psychologist Abraham Maslow developed this theory to illustrate the five levels of human needs that must be met for a person to thrive.[154] Needs lower down on the hierarchy must be satisfied before you can attend to needs higher up.

At the base of the five-tiered pyramid are the most basic physiological needs for food, water, warmth, and rest. Moving up the pyramid, there are security and safety needs, followed by belongingness and love needs (intimate relationships and friends), then esteem needs (feelings of esteem and accomplishment), and finally, self-actualization (achieving one's full potential), which is at the top of the pyramid.

As you can appreciate, security and safety needs are second only to the most basic survival functions. Obviously, you can't be concerned about personal security (e.g., running away or fighting off a predator) if your body can't physically function, just as you can't bother with creating relationships (level 3) if you're under immediate threat of harm.

Since your child's brain won't be done cooking (developing a fully functioning prefrontal cortex) until they're in their mid-20s, it's up to you, the parent, to help them fulfill those security and safety needs by teaching them what they need to know about body safety.

Remember that teaching your child about danger and how to thrive safely in the world is a process; you'll need to have ongoing conversations over the years. We only retain about 25 percent of what we read, so please consider this book to be your parenting bible—read it through to the end and refer to it often to ensure you absorb and can teach the information it contains to your child.

CHAPTER 10

Yes, No, Maybe So: Talking About Consent

I recently coached a mother whose 17-year-old daughter reluctantly confided that she had a "weird" sexual encounter with a close male friend. "Candice" had agreed to meet "Charles" at his house to play video games. His parents weren't home, but they'd been friends for years and Candice didn't think anything of it.

About an hour later, while Candice was engrossed in *World of Warcraft*, Charles put his hand on her thigh. She froze for a moment, but let it go. Then Charles leaned in for a kiss. Candice wasn't sure whether she was attracted to him... but she wasn't sure that she *wasn't* attracted to him either, so she let him kiss her.

Charles began to get more aggressive, pressing himself against her until he was on top of her on the couch. Candice was definitely not comfortable with that, but was afraid she'd hurt Charles' feelings if she told him to stop. When he began shoving his hands down her jeans, she pushed him away and said, "No," but he didn't seem to hear her.

He huskily whispered, "Let's go to my room." Again, Candice wasn't comfortable doing that, but she thought he was just fooling around and that he wouldn't push her too far (he already had); besides, the couch was really uncomfortable, and she felt trapped there.

Things escalated quickly as soon as she sat on the bed with him. Charles began furiously groping her and tearing off her clothes. Candice, a virgin, was frightened and cried, "Stop" and "No" multiple times, but he continued.

As Charles tore her jeans off, Candice froze and "checked out." Then, as she told her mom, "It just happened." After the assault, Candice numbly walked home and didn't tell anyone for days before disclosing it to her best friend.

Candice continues to blame herself for the encounter and doubts it was a genuine sexual assault, saying, "Well, yeah, I said no and all, but I DID go into his house, and then I went into his room, AND I didn't fight him off. And besides, Charles is a good guy."

I could just cry.

Yes, Candice went into Charles' house and even into his room, *but she wasn't asking to be raped!* Not only did she not give her consent, she clearly told him to stop. And that, my friends, is the most basic definition of sexual assault I can offer.

Did Charles know he was doing something wrong? Did he believe, as many guys do, that "No means yes?" Did he know he was scaring and hurting her? Was he confused himself due to his own inexperience and misconceptions about sex and intimacy?

I don't know about Charles' frame of mind on that day, and he may (or may not) be a "good guy" in every other regard, but on *that* day, he committed rape.

Candice's mom convinced her (largely against her wishes) that they had to hold him accountable. While Candice refuses to press charges (and probably wouldn't prevail in court if she did, due to the circumstances, the shitty judicial system that doesn't adequately support survivors, and the rape myths held by many people who would make up the jury), she has allowed her attorney to contact Charles' parents and demand that he take responsibility and get treatment.

Sadly, Charles continued to deny the claims and harass Candice at school and online, calling her a liar and turning others against her. She had to file a restraining order, and her parents are looking into Title IX protections at her school to limit their contact.

YES, NO, MAYBE SO: TALKING ABOUT CONSENT

Candice's story clearly shows why teaching children about consent is one of the most important jobs you have as a parent. Whether you want to keep your kid from becoming a victim or inadvertently becoming a sex offender, you want to pay super-close attention to this chapter.

How to Keep This Story From Becoming Your Kid's Reality

Sexual violence is a huge problem for tweens and teens—both as potential victims and as offenders—in part because they haven't been taught what consent means or how to ask for it.

According to the National Intimate Partner and Sexual Violence Survey Report, *more than half of all rapes of women occur before the age of 18, with 22 percent of them occurring before the age of 12!*[155]

And nearly a quarter of those arrested for sex crimes—including forcible rape, sodomy, assault with objects, and forced fondling—were under 18. The most common age was 14 years old!![156]

According to Sarah D. Sparks in her article *We're Teaching Consent All Wrong*, most kids surveyed say they've never been taught how to avoid sexually harassing others or to cope with being groped, catcalled, or bullied in sexual ways. Sixty-five percent said they wished they had received guidance on emotional aspects of relationships in their sex education classes, from how to have a mature relationship to how to deal with breakups.[157]

Well, we're going to fix that right now! Let's dive in.

Why Parents Don't Talk to Their Kids About Sex and Consent

Too many parents don't talk to their kids about sex and consent because (a) like my parents, they're "too embarrassed," (b) they don't know WHAT to say or how to say it, (c) they think their kids won't listen, (d) they fear their kids will take it as "permission" to go out and have sex, or (e) all of the above.

I'll address each one in turn:

145

- **They're too embarrassed.** Even after having two other daughters get pregnant by the age of 16, my mom and dad were still "too embarrassed" to talk to me about sex. As a result, I knew absolutely nothing about the act of sex, my body, a boy's body, birth control, sexually transmitted infections, respecting myself, setting boundaries, or consent. Zero. Zip. Nada.

So, when I began having sex at 15 (in an attempt to be cool and to get affection and attention from guys), I got pregnant almost immediately. Shockingly, after making me get an abortion, my parents STILL didn't talk to me about sex. Even more shockingly, when my younger sister went to the doctor at 18 to get on birth control before heading off to college, my mother told her she was disappointed in her! *Seriously, Mom?* The one kid of hers who was acting responsibly was shamed for making a sound choice.

Get over your embarrassment and have the talk with your kid. You can let him put a pillowcase over his head when you do it (as I did with my sons) or talk to him when you're in the car so you don't have to look each other in the eye, but *DO IT.*

If you just can't, then ask someone else you explicitly trust to have the talk with your child. When I say, "explicitly trust," that means you must be 100 percent confident that the person you choose to talk to your kid is a stand-up human being who knows about (and has demonstrated that they know about) healthy sex and relationships and isn't a potential predator.

My former brother-in-law *loved* to talk to kids about sex; he did it all time, but only as a way to groom them so he could molest them at a later time. Don't ask just anyone—your kid's coach, his Scoutmaster, etc.—just because it's convenient and lets you off the hook.

So, get over yourself and your prudish ways and *talk to your kid.* You can help him avoid so much misinformation and even trauma if you do.

- **They don't know what to say or how to say it.** There are a gazillion books on how to have the sex talk with kids. Pick one (or more). Read them. Start talking. It's pretty simple.

In actuality, it's not *A* talk, it's an ongoing conversation that starts when your child is little and should continue until they're out of college or on their own.

It's also not a bad idea to have your kid read this chapter on consent and then have a conversation with them about it when they're finished.

- **They think their kids won't listen.** I've got news for ya, 80 percent of sexually active kids never got "the talk" until AFTER they'd already started having sex, and many of them said they would have paid attention if their parents had talked with them before, during, or after they started.

This is uber important—it's not just the mom's job to have these conversations with their kids; dads need to be talking with them as well. When both parents share their perspectives with their sons and daughters, their kids will have a more well-rounded perspective about how boys and girls think and behave.

Even if your kid rolls his eyes when you broach the subjects of sex and consent, claims you're freaking him out, or pretends not to listen, *he WILL hear you* and *he really will pay attention;* he's just too embarrassed to admit it.

Like I said earlier, you can let him put a pillowcase over his head or tackle the topic when you're in a situation where you don't have to look each other in the eye. Believe me, you can get away with a lot of deep conversation on a long car ride (where he can't escape and has to listen).

Make sure you're not doing all the talking. Stop frequently to ask if he understands what you're saying or has any questions. The sooner you start these conversations, the more comfortable your kid will feel talking with you and asking those oh-so-important questions.

- **They fear their kids will take that as "permission" to go out and have sex.** This is such a myth. In fact, kids whose parents talk with them about sex often wait longer to start and have *less* sex than their peers whose parents don't.

I can tell you right now that if my parents had talked to me about healthy relationships and sex, respecting myself and my body, and how to say no when I didn't want to do something sexual, I might have waited longer to start, most likely wouldn't have gotten pregnant, and most definitely would have had sex with far fewer guys.

Start the conversation when your child is no older than 10 because kids as young as that (or even younger) are already doing it. Oh, and by the way, these days kids don't think anal or oral sex "count" as real sex and, therefore, don't take it as seriously. They're clueless about the dangers of sexually transmitted infections and pregnancy if the tip of the boy's penis so much as brushes against the girl's vaginal area. It happens.

So, to summarize, pushing through your excuses will probably result in your kid having less sex, not more, and will almost certainly ensure he or she does so in a safe, affirming way.

What Does "Consent" Actually Mean?

According to Adrienne Santos-Longhurst in her comprehensive and on-target *Healthline* article, *Your Guide to Sexual Consent*, "Consent is a voluntary, enthusiastic, and clear agreement between the participants to engage in specific sexual activity."[158]

ReachOut.com explains it this way: "Consent is when everybody involved in a sexual experience actively and freely agrees to what is happening without threat, pressure, being intoxicated, or being too young."[159]

These unambiguous definitions apply to all parties involved in any potential sexual encounter, whether it's for the first time or if they've had sex in the past (even if it was just a few minutes earlier), and regardless of their relationship status.

Sex that is *nonconsensual*—meaning one of the parties involved doesn't want it to happen and has not given consent—is rape.

Consent is also a conversation, not a onetime event. It means that each person involved in a given situation is *always* able to stop or pause any sexual activity. It also means:

- It's voluntary on the part of both parties. (BTW, repeatedly asking someone to engage in any sexual activity until they capitulate is *not* consent, nor is any sexual activity that involves fear, guilt, or pressure. *That's coercion* and it's *not* okay.)

- They're able to state what they want and don't want.

- They can change their mind at any point and have their wishes respected.

- They're awake and conscious, meaning they're not too incapacitated by drugs or alcohol to make a rational decision about what they want and to express that. Failure to recognize or acknowledge that someone is too impaired to consent is not "drunk sex"; it's rape.

- They understand what kinds of activity they're agreeing to, which also means they have the mental capacity to understand what's happening. People with developmental disabilities are too often the victims of sexual encounters they don't understand or have the ability to decline.

- They're over the legal age for sexual consent. Ages vary by state, and your child needs to know what the age is in your state so they don't get charged with statutory rape.

When you talk to your kid early and often about getting and giving consent, she's far more likely to have healthy, respectful relationships and safe and enjoyable sexual experiences when she's ready for them.

And isn't that the best we could possibly wish for our kids? I mean, really, what's more important than that? You can help make that wish come true for your child by talking with her about it.

Doing so from the time she's little (in an age-appropriate way, of course) sends the message that you're a reliable, approachable resource for information and advice about sex. If she grows up feeling comfortable talking to you when she's 10, she'll be more likely to come to you when she's 15 and 18.

Trust me; you want this.

How Is Consent Conveyed?

In any super-sexy, sweaty, emotionally arousing amorous encounter, when hormones are raging at their peak and everything just feels *so damn good*, it can be hard for anyone to be objective enough to pay attention to the little things like, "Is she also totally into this?" or "Am I okay to proceed?" But it's not impossible and you need to teach your kid to make it a habit to frequently check in with his partner when things get hot and heavy.

Tweens and teens are *really* bad at making decisions involving risky behavior, especially when under pressure in sexual situations and especially if they feel like they "have to" do it or they'll be judged by their peers or bullied for being a "wuss," "frigid," a "tease," or a "bitch."

It's important to be straight with your kid, especially your daughter, about the kinds of sexual pressure she might be subjected to. Too many girls have heard something along the lines of, "Take off your clothes; I promise I won't try anything," or "Let me just put the tip in; I promise I won't go all the way," only to have the situation get completely out of hand.

Again, for those who missed it, like, two minutes ago—just "putting the tip in" can lead to pregnancy. Boys' bodies prepare themselves for sexual encounters by releasing a little bit of sperm to make penetration easier. Your kid needs to know this.

Back to the topic of sexual pressure.

Most kids WAY overestimate the quantity and quality of the sex their peers are having. Knowing (because you tell them so) that most of it is pure BS and wishful thinking meant to impress their friends will help take the pressure off them to "perform." Encourage them to worry less about what their friends and peers think and more about what they think about themselves and their partners.

Does your son want to see himself as respectful of others (especially women and girls)? As kind? As smart? As not a total douche canoe? Encourage him to actually BE those things by following his head and heart and not his, well, you know.

What to Teach Your Kid About Consent

Asking for consent is actually super easy and not as much of a turnoff as you'd think. Teach your kid to actually talk to the person they're into *before* initiating any sexual activity.

Note: Below, I'm going to use second-person pronouns as if I were speaking directly to your kid. Again, I recommend you have your tween or teen read this chapter and then have a conversation about it with you to ensure they're able to ask any questions they have and so you can dispel any confusion about what I share here.

Here goes.

Women and girls are more cerebral than men, and most of the time the way to win them over is first through their minds and *then* through their bodies. Think of it as emotional foreplay, guys.

It's the responsibility of the person initiating the sexual activity to ensure their partner feels safe and comfortable. Start by asking, "What are you into/comfortable with right now?" Let them know you don't want to do anything they're not 100 percent okay with.

You can actually turn securing consent into foreplay and a hot part of your sexual experience. Once your partner has agreed to the first move, usually in the form of a hug or kiss, check in with them before moving to the next level by asking, "Is it okay to...?" or "Are you cool with...?"

As you proceed and things get hotter, ask: "Do you like this?" "It feels so good when you (fill in the blank); do you want to do this?" "Can I take your clothes off?" "Can I kiss you here?" Or (especially if you sense any hesitancy), "Are you comfortable with me doing this?"

And before initiating any sex act, be sure to ask, "Do you want to give me a hand job/go down on me/have sex, or would you like to wait?"

Then be prepared for the answer and respect it.

151

If your partner seems hesitant or expresses any of the verbal or nonverbal cues I list in the section below on Indicators of Nonconsent, *STOP.* Move back from them physically and give them some space to breathe. Take a break and check in with them.

Ask: "Are you okay? Do you want me to stop?" AND "What's going on in your mind right now?" This last question is a particularly good one to ask because it's open-ended and will encourage your partner to share what they're really thinking at that moment.

If they're into what's been happening, this is their chance to let you know. If they're NOT into it, they'll either say so at this point or equivocate, using language that kinda, sorta means stop, in which case, you *STOP.*

If you're just not sure whether they're okay with what's happening... *STOP.* Take a step back from the situation and let things cool down. Be sure to let your partner know you're okay with not going any farther.

Yes, it means you may end up feeling sexually and emotionally frustrated when they ask you to slow down or stop, but you'll have the reward of knowing you were respectful of your partner's needs and that you didn't go on to commit what may have turned into a sexual offense that you—and they—might have regretted later.

Remember, it's important to check in with your partner, even if you've done the same thing (or more) in the past and even if you're in a long-term, committed relationship.

Fully embrace the truth that no one *owes* you sex, just as you don't *owe* it to anyone to engage in any sexual activity you're not okay with, even if the other person is your girlfriend/boyfriend and even if they threaten to end the relationship if you don't "put out."

Hang on; I gotta stop here for a sec to address all the young girls who desperately believe that if they don't let the guy they're with go all the way (or do something sexual that they're really not comfortable with), then he'll break up with them and they'll not only lose the attention and affection they crave, but also the social status that comes with having a boyfriend.

Know that most young guys falsely believe that every other guy is getting laid on a regular basis and that they have to "score" too in order to keep up their image. They're not, and they don't.

At the same time, many girls believe that they *have* to put out in order to be loved (or popular, or cool... you get my drift). Been there, done that, got the boy's class ring to prove it.

But here's the truth: Any guy who genuinely cares for you would never want to hurt you sexually or emotionally. Recognize that they may not know themself what's appropriate in a sexual encounter or what you need to feel comfortable. Recognize too that guys are not mind readers. You have to be *explicitly* clear with your partner about what you're into and where your boundaries are, even when it's embarrassing or difficult to resist.

Honey, sugar, sweetie. Trust me, if this guy is the one for you, he'll respect your boundaries and wait until (if/when) you're ready. If he's not willing to wait and tries to pressure you into sexual activity you're not comfortable with, he 100 percent is NOT the one for you!

The guy who IS the one for you is out there, making his way toward you. Be patient; the two of you *will* find each other.

What Consent Is

Consent can be verbal ("Yes, I want this, please continue.") or nonverbal (e.g., thumbs up, nodding yes, pulling you toward them, pleasurable moaning, arching of the back). However, moaning in and of itself could indicate pain or displeasure and the arching of the back could also be a way of trying to push someone away.

Needless to say, it's confusing.

Sexual consent is necessary in any situation between two or more[xxvi] people that involves:

* Kissing
* Touching someone in a sexual way on any part of their body

---

xxvi What can I say? Sex isn't always just one-on-one, and your kid needs to know that, even in group situations, consent must be given by each person involved.

- Sending sexual messages or images
- Having vaginal, oral, or anal sex (or any activity that involves the sexual organs)
- Not using condoms or other forms of contraception

If you want to do any of the above with another person, you *must* ensure the other person clearly wants it to happen.

If you're on the receiving end of these kinds of activities, remember that it's okay to say no before or while the activity is occurring, and that you have a right and even a responsibility to let the other person know what you do and do not want to happen. It's okay to say things such as, "I like you, but I'm not ready" or "No, not yet."

Because I was so clueless about sex and had never even heard of the idea of consent when I was a teen, I ended up in too many situations where I truly didn't want to kiss/hug/touch/be touched/have sex with other people but did so *because I didn't know I didn't have to.*

I actually thought I *owed* it to guys to follow through with sex if I let them kiss me or I was being a "tease." I often dreaded dates because of the impending kiss and inevitable sex that was almost sure to follow. Not surprisingly, I got a reputation as a total ho in high school, but it was inadvertent and not willful.

Nevertheless, because I often didn't say no or let my partners know I wasn't comfortable moving forward, none of those encounters could be considered sexual assault.

Again, guys are not mind readers, and it's easy to misinterpret nonverbal cues (like when a partner pulls back, withdraws, or becomes silent).

Many young men are socialized or actively taught (by equally clueless friends, "well-meaning" dads, or totally unrealistic porn) to believe that women like to be conquered or seduced (some do, and that's okay too *if* it's a real choice), that dressing provocatively is "asking for it," that girls will put up resistance only because they don't want to seem "easy," or that No really means Yes.

None of these is true, but those ideas are still hanging out there in many kids' minds. THAT'S why it's so important to talk to your child about consent and not assume he knows what it is. Trust me, if you don't talk to him, he'll get his information from those equally clueless friends or godawful porn sites, and then he'll have a totally screwed-up idea of what's appropriate and respectful in sexual encounters.

Indicators of Non-Consent

Here are some things consent definitely is NOT:[160]

- Saying, "No," "I don't want that," "I'm not ready," "Stop," "That hurts," "I don't want to do this anymore," "This feels wrong," etc.
- Less clear, but also meaning No are, "I want to, but...," "I'm not sure," "I don't know," "I feel worried about...," "Maybe," "I love you, but...," "I don't know how I feel about this," etc.
- Silence on the part of the person the sexual acts are being done to (the absence of a clear No doesn't mean Yes)
- Avoiding eye contact
- Not initiating any sexual activity
- Not removing their own clothing
- Pushing the person away or avoiding their touch
- Crying or looking sad or fearful
- Shaking their head
- Closed body language (e.g., being tense, stiff, having a frozen expression, turning away)
- Just lying there (again, the absence of a clear No doesn't mean Yes)

In addition to these, the person initiating the sexual activity should not be in a position of authority or trust over his partner, such as a doctor, clergyman, teacher, employer, or coach.

I'll say it loud for the people in back: If you're not sure whether the person you're with is into it, *STOP*.

If you ask most women (and every single woman I've asked has admitted this), they'll say they've had sex when they really didn't want to, often giving in to get it over with and not because they were consenting to whatever "it" was.

A Word About Consent Under the Influence of Drugs or Alcohol

Many kids under the legal age drink or do drugs. You may not want to believe YOUR kid does, but you just don't know for sure, do ya?

Being buzzed or even drunk or drugged doesn't always mean a person isn't coherent enough to provide consent, but it sure makes it more difficult to gauge. Research shows a direct relationship between excessive alcohol consumption and the risk of committing sexual assault.[161] In about half of all rapes, either the perp, the victim, or both were under the influence of alcohol.[162]

To be clear, if a person is raped when drunk or under the influence of drugs, it's *never* their fault. Their "partners" (assailants) took advantage of the situation (whether or not they were drunk or on drugs themselves). Unfortunately, many law enforcement officers, courts, and jury members don't see it that way, blaming the victim for being irresponsible.

If either person in a given sexual encounter is under the influence, it becomes even more important to ensure consent is explicitly offered— and only when they're certain that person is capable of making a rational choice (meaning they're not so impaired they don't know what they're doing or will likely regret it later).

Here are some clear indicators that a person isn't able to give meaningful consent:

- They're fumbling, stumbling, or can't stand without help. Just because they fall into your arms or lean on you so they don't fall down doesn't mean they're asking for sex.
- They're slurring their words, dropping things, or falling asleep.

- They've been vomiting.
- They're behaving recklessly and aren't making good choices.

Even if you're certain the other person is in good enough shape to agree to engage in sexual activity, if they're buzzed or high you should still ask, "Do you feel clear enough to be making decisions about sex right now?"[163] But regardless of what they say in response to your question, if YOU think they're not in any condition to make that decision, you need to stop right there.

How to Teach Your Kid About Consent

When teaching your kid about consent, start right away at whatever age *they* are now, whether that's two or 12. In my last books for those with kids zero to nine, *Badass Parenting* and *Heroic Parenting*, I teach parents about the importance of talking to their kids from diapers on about body autonomy, setting and defending physical and emotional boundaries, saying no to anyone who makes them uncomfortable, and trusting and acting on their intuition.

These topics are just as important and relevant for tweens and teens and you shouldn't despair if you're just now broaching them.

Here are some things you can teach your kid that will help them understand and appreciate consent:

- Anytime they engage with another person, pay attention to how that person is reacting to ensure they're not feeling uncomfortable or afraid.
- Keep an eye on the other person's facial expressions and body language for clues that they're uncomfortable with whatever's happening, and stop if you sense something's off.
- Don't do stupid shit that crosses physical boundaries. This could range from slapping someone's butt to snapping a girl's bra strap. Boys, especially younger ones, think it's funny to touch and provoke girls they like, but the girls don't appreciate it one bit.

- Don't cross emotional boundaries by making catcalls, sexual remarks, or innuendos, calling someone a slut or whore to be "funny," or commenting on someone's body (either in a positive or negative way).

- Learn to recognize and respect other people's feelings, physical and emotional boundaries, and wishes. Let them know this is true across the board, whether it's with their best bro, grandmother, or girlfriend/boyfriend.

- In turn, show them that you respect their feelings, physical and emotional boundaries, and wishes, and make certain others do the same. You do this by not forcing them to hug or kiss Grandpa or allowing others to violate their personal space. Call people out on it when you see it and encourage your kid to do the same.

- Have your child choose a safe word to use with friends and love interests that ensures any activity comes to a full stop. Pick something silly like "meatball" or "octopus" or something serious like "Knock it off!" or "I really mean it!" Obviously, they need to tell their friend/love interest what the safe word is in advance.

- Continue having regular talks with them about sex, consent, and the consequences of their choices.

- Tell them that physical arousal doesn't always mean they're into what's happening. Our bodies are weird, mysterious beings that have minds of their own and sometimes act counter to our wishes. Explicitly say, "Just because you had an erection/were wet down there doesn't mean you were ready for sex or wanted it."

- Anytime they're engaging with another person in a sexual way, they need to ensure that person isn't:
  - Incapacitated by drugs or alcohol
  - Developmentally impaired or disabled
  - Of an inappropriate age
  - Being coerced by the initiator's size, age, or position of authority

- Encourage your child to think critically and creatively by asking such questions as, "How can you tell if a girl is interested in you?"

or "What would you do if someone tried to kiss you, but you didn't want them to?"

- Teach them that rejection, including sexual rejection, is a part of life that everyone experiences, and that it's not the end of the world.

- Teach them how their brain works and is still forming (Google it for your child's age). Just knowing that their raging hormones may account for their moodiness, horniness, and insecurity can be reassuring.

- Talk about the effects and consequences of using drugs and alcohol (including the fact that it makes them less able to offer consent or recognize the signs of nonconsent, and that it makes them more likely to be taken advantage of). Make it clear you don't want them drinking or doing drugs, but if they do, they need to be responsible (both in terms of their behavior and the consequences they'll face as a result).

- Role-play a variety of scenarios with them. For example, ask them how they'd know whether it's okay to engage in sexual activity with someone who's been drinking, or what they would do if someone touched them in a way they didn't like, up to and including their girlfriend/boyfriend.

- Acknowledge how much harder it is to say no to people they like, love, work for, and/or respect. Reassure them that those people will almost always stop whatever's making them feel uncomfortable if they ask them to. Emphasize that if the other person *doesn't* stop the offending behavior, your kid should yell and get away from them as quickly as possible, and then tell you what happened so you can ensure it doesn't happen again.

- PLEASE talk with your kid about pornography. Tell them it's not realistic and that it incorrectly portrays women as sex-starved vixens and men as conquering studs. Let them know that it's actually damaging to their psyche and can impact their ability to engage in healthy sexual relationships.

- Speaking of which, talk with your kid about healthy sexual relationships. Seventy percent of 18- to 25-year-old respondents surveyed said they wish they'd received more information from their parents about what healthy relationships look like.[166] Many kids, your kid included, want to know how to begin a relationship, how to end one, how to deal with breakups, and how to navigate dating relationships and sex.

• When your kid starts "talking" with or dating someone, have an extra-special conversation with them about what a healthy relationship looks like and reassert your views on consent.

Make certain your kid knows they can come to you with any questions or problems, even if they've broken the rules. Give them a "get out of jail free[xxvii]" card they can use to call or talk to you about a poor choice they've made or something bad that's happened to them without you freaking out and punishing them until you're heard the full story and have had time to cool down.

During this cooling-off period, your job is just to listen and ask gentle questions to draw the full story out of them. Your first duty is to ensure they're safe. That may mean picking them up from a raging party where they drank too much or giving them a shoulder to cry on if their girlfriend/ boyfriend went too far sexually.

The "not freaking out" part may be super hard, but it's essential. If your child thinks you'll lose it (by putting them on restriction for the entire summer, as my parents once did, or by threatening to "kill" the other person), they won't tell you anything and you won't be able to help or guide them.

You want your kid to feel comfortable coming to you, and honestly, they do too. You can help build that kind of trust with your tween or teen if you're consistently there for them and keep your cool when they tell you something that makes your hair turn white.

---

xxvii You can download a special "Get out of jail FREE" card when you sign up for my FREEBIES page on my website at www.cjscarlet.com. Your kid can keep this card in their wallet or handbag to give back to you when they need you to reserve judgment and hear them out.

Badass Grandma's Two Cents

I wrote much of this chapter using they/them pronouns because everything here applies to both boys and girls. Girls are most often the victims of nonconsensual sex but can also be the offenders. It's important they understand both sides of the equation.

I'll say it one more time: It's a good idea to let your kid read this chapter on consent and then talk with them about what they learned. They should have lots of questions at this point that you'll want to carefully consider and answer.

If you don't know the answer or they ask a question that freaks you out, you can always say something like, "Hmmm, I'm not sure about that. Let me think about it and get back to you." Then do your research so can give them a proper response.

Don't wait too long between their question and your answer, so they know you took them seriously. (If you're really stumped, you can always email me at cj@cjscarlet.com. I offer virtual coaching for parents.)

Finally, I want to reiterate that these conversations need to come from BOTH Mom AND Dad. Each of you can offer a unique perspective based on your gender that your son or daughter will benefit from.

The gift of the conversations you have with your kid around this topic will help ensure they make sound choices throughout their life. Good for you for stepping up and being the influencer they need while they learn to navigate those tricky relationship waters.

CHAPTER 11

Teaching Your Kid About Body Safety

Your kid is morphing so fast in every way, from their body and mind to their emotions, that it's hard to keep up with them. As they begin to deal with all the confusing physical and mental changes that come with puberty and young adulthood, they can be mercurial at best and a total freaking shitshow at worst.

Your kid may have lots of energy and interests, or she may prefer to curl up with a good book or play video games in her free time. She probably is now paying more attention to the latest trends in music and fashion and likes to wear her hair a certain way. She may be into sleepovers and hanging out with friends, which means you need to ensure you've taught her how to set and enforce strong physical and emotional boundaries and about what to do if she finds herself in an uncomfortable or potentially abusive situation.

Your kid can also be super responsible one minute and then pitch a screaming fit worthy of a three-year-old in need of a nap the next, making it hard to gauge how much you can trust her to do what's in her own best interest.

Every kid needs (and secretly wants) rules to guide them and keep them safe. They also need to know the consequences of breaking those rules, and you, the parent, need to be consistent in applying them. Trust me; no one can find a loophole in a social contract faster than a kid. If you let your child get away with breaking a fast-and-firm family rule just one time, you'll never hear the end of it if you later try to punish her for doing the same thing.

Don't let her tirades or tantrums wear you down or you've just taught her that if she cries, threatens, or badgers you long enough, she'll get her way. That is seriously bad juju for you and a total win for her.

Having said that, your kid wants to know *why* particular rules are important. "Because I said so" isn't a satisfying answer AND it's a total cop-out. Tell her, firmly, that your rules are meant to keep her safe and that even when she thinks they're not important or relevant, you, as the parent, have a responsibility to protect her.

Having said THAT, sometimes it works, sometimes it doesn't. I myself have resorted to the old standby, "My house, my rules. When you pay the bills, you can help make the decisions." My kids never had a good comeback for that one other than stomping off and not speaking to me for several blissfully quiet hours.

Remember, your kid's prefrontal cortex, the part of the brain that controls impulses, doesn't finish developing until she's in her mid-20s. In other words, don't be surprised if she lacks impulse control when it comes to using her smartphone and navigating relationships.

When the Puberty Bomb Goes Off

Your kid's biggest obsession—above and beyond even getting a smartphone—is, "Am I normal?" Kids don't physically develop at the same rate, and this can devastate their confidence and self-esteem.

According to the Sexuality Resource Center (whose srcp.org website has apparently been taken over by an injectable steroid distribution company from China, so I'm not able to give you the original source), "If you're the first girl in your class to develop breasts, that's a bad thing. If you're the last girl in your class to develop breasts, that's a bad thing. If you're a boy who gets an erection in front of the class, that's a bad thing. If you're a boy whose voice cracks when you're trying to impress a girl, that's a bad thing. Getting your period when you're not prepared – bad. If you're a boy, and all the girls are taller than you – bad. Uncontrollable mood swings for both girls and boys – bad. The variations are almost endless. Throw in pimples and body odor, and you can begin to understand why puberty can be such a tough time for pre-teens and teens."

Jesus on a jet ski! Memories of my own pubescent nightmares are making me want to gouge my eyes out with a pointy object. I truly feel for your kids, my grandkids, and *every* kid who has to go through this.

Bend over backward to convince your growing child that they ARE normal and that they'll eventually get through it. They need to know they're not alone and that every single kid on the planet has anxiety and self-doubt at this point... yes, even the most popular cheerleaders and cutest boys in their class.

If you don't know the answer to a question your kid asks or have questions or concerns of your own about what's appropriate behavior, talk with your pediatrician.

What Your Kid Needs From You

Your child wants soooo much to be older than she is and can't wait to officially become an adult, but she's really still a child in many ways. Just know that she won't be as open to that cutsie nickname you always called her (even Honey Boo Boo grew up eventually), and she won't like being teased about things such as her appearance or secret crushes.

Personal privacy becomes an issue as kids age, and you want to respect that. However, you also need to ensure you're staying vigilant about her behavior when it comes to her phone (if she has one yet) and online activities (including video games). Be sure to read, and even reread, Chapter 7 on Online Dangers so you can talk to her about what those dangers are and how to handle herself in sketchy situations.

She (hopefully) still thinks you have many of the answers, although she looks more and more to her peers to decide how to act, dress, and even think. These peer relationships will become increasingly influential, so it's important to make the conversations you have with her count. But peer cliques are constantly fluctuating and sometimes your kid will be excluded, which is painful (for you both).

It becomes even tougher as your child struggles to develop her unique identity while at the same time trying to fit in with the "normal" or popular kids. Honestly, your kid has no clue who she is, what she really believes, and where she fits in.

And that's okay. That's what life is all about—figuring all that out. That's HER job, and she'll do it by experimenting with boundaries and relationships and, potentially, things like drugs, alcohol, or sex.

YOUR job is to support and encourage her to make sound choices, help her set and enforce solid boundaries, and to act as a bumper she can bang against as she navigates the relationships and situations around her.

BTW, if you think she's too young to even *consider* trying drugs or alcohol or engaging in sexual activity, *YOU'RE WRONG*. Kids as young as 10 (and even younger) are being pressured by their peers to try these things, and most kids will have a hard time saying no.

Kids want attention and affection like everyone else, and they're desperate to gain the approval of their peers. Unfortunately, often the way they try to fit in is by getting a boyfriend or girlfriend.

Young girls who are desperate for a boyfriend, or who want to avoid losing one to another girl who *will* "put out," may do things they're not ready for or comfortable with. They may believe everyone does it, and they may be close to right because it *is* happening at an alarming rate.

As long as we're on the topic of sex...

Let's Talk About Sex, Baybee!

If you haven't already started having conversations with your child about her body, how it works, how boys' bodies work, what puberty means and what changes will occur, what healthy intimate relationships look like, what's appropriate in a relationship at her age, how babies are *really* made, and so on, *definitely start NOW*.

You can bet she's hearing all manner of nonsense from her friends (and potentially, online porn sites), and you want to ensure you're in her head, so to speak, to counter any balderdash with a large dose of reality and perspective.

Trust me when I tell you that she has a million questions about these and other topics that she'd love the answers to but is probably afraid or too shy to ask. It's up to you to broach those subjects (in a non-pushy way, of course), so she can ask away while feeling safe and comfortable. (Okay, maybe not *comfortable,* but at least feeling like she can speak freely.)

It's really important not to judge, ridicule, or tease her if she asks silly or naïve questions—even when they're super funny or shocking. If you accidentally embarrass or shame her, she'll likely clam up and any chance you have of teaching her the truth will be lost. Instead, say something like, "Yes, I can see why you might think kissing can get you pregnant, but that's not how it works. Let's talk about how it really happens."

You'll want to stress to your child that once puberty begins, girls (who've started their periods) are able to get pregnant and boys (because they're now producing sperm) are capable of getting someone pregnant.

Oh, and she's probably going to be regularly masturbating (for boys, remove the "probably" part of that sentence). As long as she keeps it private, there's usually nothing to worry about.

The More They Know, the Safer They Are

I already covered this in the chapter on consent but humor me as I say it once again—many parents are afraid that if they talk with their kids about sex, it will encourage them to "do it." In reality, though, kids are more likely to delay sexual activity when they know the facts and are taught about boundaries and consent. *AND* these kids are far less likely to be victimized by sexual predators who are looking to exploit naïve young people who are unsure of what's what.

The National Child Traumatic Stress Network assures parents that it's a myth that talking about sex with their child will encourage them to become sexually active. Its website notes that in a recent survey of American teens, nine out of 10 said it would be easier to delay sexual activity and prevent unwanted pregnancy if they were able to have "more open, honest conversations" with their parents on these topics.[165]

According to StopItNow.org,[166] "Having ongoing conversations with your children and teens about their own developing sexuality is an important part of sexual abuse prevention. Early messages that sex and sexuality are shameful or not to be discussed can lead to children keeping secrets about sexual touching."

This StopItNow.org article goes on to list several key reasons why healthy sexuality education should be an important part of your family's safety plan:

- It communicates your willingness to discuss sexual issues with your kid and lets them know they can turn to you when they feel confused or have questions.
- By feeling safe to talk with you about sex and sexuality, kids are more likely to tell you if they've been harmed or if they've been engaging in troubling behaviors.
- Encouraging your kid to speak openly with you about sexual concerns helps counteract the secrecy needed to hide sexually abusive behaviors.
- Healthy sexuality education makes it more likely that kids will understand when they need help and then seek that help from an adult.
- Discussions help define safe social, physical, and sexual boundaries for kids who might be confused or otherwise act in inappropriate or harmful ways.
- It shows your tween or teen that they can rely on you for accurate information. Because we live in a culture where we're exposed to confusing and misleading sexual imagery and information, this is particularly important.
- Holding honest and respectful discussions about sexual issues gives you the opportunity to impart your values to your children.

So, to recap, talking early and often about sex with your kid will help protect her and make it more likely she'll make good choices when it comes to intimate relationships.

Here are some conversation starters you can use to get your tween or teen to open up to you:

- "You must be excited about your date with Julian tonight. He seems really nice. What are some things you like about him?"
- "Being in a relationship can sometimes get tricky. I'm always here if you ever want to chat about how things are going."
- "I want to make sure you know that it's always okay to stop sexual activity you both initially wanted—at any point. Even if your boy-friend/girlfriend says it's not fair to them for you to change your mind, your feelings and safety always come first."

A Word About Sexual Orientation

At this point in their lives, kids may ask a lot of questions about sexual orientation and probably have a head full of misinformation about the topic. Today's kids are much more open and accepting of LGBTQIA+ lifestyles and issues and are more likely to explore different orientations themselves.

It helps to educate yourself first about the various sexual orientations and issues so you can talk intelligently about them if your child expresses an interest in this area. There are a ton of books for both kids and parents on these topics that will help you broach them in an affirming, nonjudg-mental manner.

Above all, I beg of you, support your kid if he or she tells you they iden-tify as queer.

Love is love, y'all.

What to Teach Your Kid to Keep Him Safe

There are a gazillion things you could teach your kid about body safety, but to make it super easy for you, I'm going to teach you the three most important skills he should cultivate to protect himself from emotional and physical harm.

I call them "superpowers" because kids who practice them are better at spotting danger and avoiding it before it escalates.

The three superpowers are:

1. His boundaries
2. His intuition
3. His moxie

Teaching Your Kid to Honor His Intuition

Your child's first and most important superpower is his intuition—or gut. His body is a finely tuned instrument of wisdom and knowing. It's constantly giving him cues about his environment and the people in it. Some of these cues, which you can teach your child to watch for, include:

- A feeling of wariness or foreboding
- A nagging feeling that something isn't right
- Feelings of panic or anxiety
- Fear or apprehension
- A sense of doubt or hesitancy
- A sick or sinking feeling in his stomach
- Feelings that make the hair on the back of his neck and arms stand up, just as it does in animals who sense something threatening in their environment
- Rapid, shallow breathing
- A pounding heart
- A rushing sensation in his ears or head
- Tunnel vision
- Difficulty hearing

Teach your kid to trust that when these sensations appear, something isn't right in his environment and he needs to act IMMEDIATELY to remove himself from the situation, even if it means being rude to an adult or another kid.

That may mean excusing himself to use the bathroom and sneaking out the back door to escape, or it may mean forcefully yelling at the offender to back off. Teach him to do *whatever* it takes to honor his intuition and protect himself.

Acting on His Intuition

Tell your kid that he shouldn't give someone the benefit of the doubt if he feels uncomfortable around them. Teach him to challenge them in whatever way is appropriate at that moment, whether it's warning them to stop the offending behavior and running away, yelling for help, or fighting like a rabid Tasmanian devil (outlined in Chapter 14). Give your kid free reign to do what's necessary to stop the offender and get away from him (or her) as fast as possible.

The more in tune your kid is with his inner voice, the more quickly he'll recognize and listen to it when he needs it. When it tells him to be careful or to do something differently, teach him to heed that voice! It's his best friend and it won't steer him wrong.

Acting on YOUR Intuition

Your intuition is your first line of defense when protecting your child. You need to pay attention when it tells you a particular person isn't to be trusted, even when the rest of the world insists there's nothing wrong.

When your radar or your child's indicates that a particular person is "iffy," do NOT ignore that warning! One way to handle a situation where a person creeps your child out (but hasn't done anything overtly inappropriate) is to talk to that person.

By saying something as simple as: "Devon doesn't like it when you try to wrestle with him. Please don't do that anymore," you're putting the offender on notice that he's being watched, which will almost certainly cause him to write your kid off as a target.

If you're not comfortable talking to the person by yourself, you can ask another adult or someone in authority to be there with you. Or, if you're really chicken, you can have that other person talk to them for you. Do whatever you need to do to deliver the message that the offender needs to back off.

My personal preference in this situation is to ensure your kid never has to be around anyone who makes him uncomfortable or afraid, to be certain he remains safe. I'm not kidding here; I literally broke off all contact with my entire family for 11 years because I didn't want to expose my sons to predatory family members.

This Badass Grandma don't play.

A Word on the Importance of Situational Awareness

Put simply, situational awareness means your kid knows what's going on around him. Not having it means he's clueless and a bull's-eye for predators. Perps are generally opportunistic; they tend to look for victims they consider easy marks, and many crimes are crimes of opportunity, meaning predators seize the chance to molest or assault a child because the opportunity is there and there's a good chance they won't be caught.

Kids are automatically considered vulnerable targets by perps because they're young, innocent, and trusting. Plus, they often aren't paying attention to what's going on around them. Awareness of his environment and the people around him is a necessary life skill you must teach your child and have him practice so it becomes second nature.

Your kid's awareness feeds his gut information it needs to decide whether he's safe or not. When his intuition is triggered, he needs to laser-focus on what the problem is. If he can't discern any obvious reason for his gut reaction, tell him to trust it anyway and remove himself from the situation.

Setting and Defending Personal Boundaries

The second superpower consists of your child's boundaries, which represent the line he allows people to cross (or not) in his physical and emotional space. While intuition is an innate sense that can be cultivated to protect him from danger, establishing and defending boundaries are skills that must be learned and practiced if they are to become effective.

Healthy boundaries look like a circle, with your child in the middle (as the person he most trusts), surrounded by a slightly larger circle that he saves for you and his closest friends and loved ones, and then outer circles for acquaintances and people he doesn't know. On the outer limits, outside all the circles, are people he doesn't trust.

When talking about this with your kid, actually draw these circles and have him name where people go on the drawing. It might surprise you who he chooses to put on the outer limits, which should prompt you to ask why he doesn't trust these people. *I strongly urge you to do this exercise with your kid; it can reveal people or situations in your child's life that make him uncomfortable or that are actually abusive.*

Unhealthy boundaries are vague and, in some cases, may be totally missing in action. I think of it as a watercolor painting; the edges are blurry and undefined. People with wobbly boundaries bleed into other people, and others bleed into them. This is often the case for those who've been victimized by people they should have been able to trust. When a child is abused, his boundaries become confused, leading him to either not trust anyone or to allow everyone to trample them.

You are your kid's best teacher in this area. Your job is to talk with him about boundaries and help him decide what his are, and then teach him how to recognize when they're being violated and how to defend them. The rest of the world will reinforce what you teach him by testing his boundaries on a regular basis. If you've done a good job with your role, these lessons from the rest of the world will be instructive rather than traumatic.

Predators WILL test a potential victim's boundaries to determine whether he'll make a good target. They may first attempt to cross his emotional boundaries by making suggestive or inappropriate comments or jokes to see how he reacts. If he smiles nervously or freezes and doesn't react, the predator will often push further in an attempt to manipulate him into a bad situation.

If someone crosses a physical or emotional boundary with your child, you want him to know how to stop the offender in their tracks—whether it's a stranger or someone he knows well. A simple, "Stop. I don't like that," may be all it takes.

Tell your child not to be afraid of being wrong or looking silly. When he tells someone to back off and give him space, if the offender's a good guy, he'll do it and probably apologize. If he's a predator, he might get angry with your kid and try to make him feel bad about setting a boundary. This is your child's cue that this person is not to be trusted and to get away from them as fast as his legs can carry him.

How to Respond to Boundary Violations

Here are some polite but firm responses to boundary violations you can teach your child to use:

- "No, thank you."
- "You're standing too close. Please back up a bit."
- "I don't want to sit on your lap."
- "Please don't touch me. That's not okay."
- "I don't like that. Please stop."
- "Don't do that."
- "No!"
- "Stop!"

Your child can use these simple phrases to set boundaries any time someone makes him feel uncomfortable. Knowing he has permission to tell others no, including adults and authority figures, gives him tremendous power and advantage.

Often, reinforcing a boundary like that with a perp who's trying to groom him lets that person know he's not going to meekly comply and is very likely to tell on him. That's the last thing the predator wants, so he'll most likely stop the offending behavior.

How to Teach Your Kid About Boundaries

As you educate your kid about his boundaries and how to defend them, also teach him to honor other people's boundaries. This means, for example, asking others for permission before giving hugs or touching them, allowing

TEACHING YOUR KID ABOUT BODY SAFETY

them privacy in the bathroom and bedroom, and stopping a particular behavior when asked to do so.

In the previous chapter, I shared how to teach your child about consent. Please refer to that chapter for more on this subject.

Your Child's Moxie

Your kid's third superpower is his moxie, also called "nerve" or "chutzpah." It's your child's willingness to stand in his power to honor his intuition and defend his boundaries. It means summoning his inner badass and walking his talk. It means being as rude or aggressive as necessary to someone who's setting off alarm bells in his body and pushing his boundaries past the breaking point.

If you read the Introduction (if you didn't, shame on you; go read it now), I talked about helping your child stay "left of bang," which means teaching him how to avoid danger before it escalates. Below are some phrases and nonphysical actions he can use to verbally de-escalate and extract himself from a given situation (like being pressured to have sex or to try drugs or alcohol, for example):

- I wish I could, but I have to write a paper tonight.
- I have an exam tomorrow I need to study for.
- No, thanks (for the drink/drugs); I'm the designated driver.
- No, thanks. I've reached my limit.
- Sorry, I have a game tomorrow and want to be at my best, so I don't want to be out late.
- I have plans already.
- I wish I could (have a drink/drugs), but I'm on medication.
- My parents would kill me.
- I don't feel comfortable with that.
- No, I'm not ready to take that step yet.
- Sorry, I'm on my period.
- No. (Enough said.)

- Stop!
- Help!
- Get away!
- I'm going to call the police if you don't stop. (And then DO IT if they don't stop.)

If all else fails and an assault is imminent, your kid needs to know how to physically defend himself. In Chapter 14, I share how to teach your child to fight like a rabid Tasmanian devil—using his own body as a weapon—which doesn't require any formal martial arts or self-defense training.

These are seriously crucial skills he (and even you!) needs to learn if you're both to feel confident that he can handle himself in potentially dangerous situations.

Give Your Kid a Fighting Chance

Let me stop here for a moment and address those of my readers who are thinking, "My child is too young/nice/polite/timid/afraid/insert your own objection here."

All that may be true, but you've got to give your kid a fighting chance! Teach him what he needs to know about how to recognize and act on his intuition and keep emphasizing how to take action if he needs to.

He's more likely to repel creepy people when he knows about boundaries and intuition than if you don't teach him anything about them. At the very least, even if he freezes and doesn't react in the moment to protect himself, he'll be more likely to tell you if something bad happens. Makes sense, right?

Teach your kid to THINK about what he's doing before he hugs that person or obeys the command of a peer or adult who gives him that "uh-oh" feeling in his stomach. Tell him to check in with his intuition and the clues his body is giving him first. He doesn't owe it to anyone to do what they want, even if they're persistent (and bad guys will be persistent).

If he feels okay about doing whatever it is he's considering, and it aligns with his intuition and integrity, he can choose to do it. If it doesn't resonate with him and he has doubts, he shouldn't do it. It's that simple.

When to Teach Your Kid About Body Safety Issues

If you want your kid to pay attention to you when you talk with him about body safety issues, choose a time when you're both comfortable and relaxed. Trying to talk when either of you is stressed is a bad idea.

Consider the following times to have a conversation about body safety with your child:

- **Before he heads out.** Before your kid goes off to a sleepover, to the mall with friends, or on a date, go over your safety rules. For example, say, "Remember to text me when you get there and let me know if you find yourself in a tricky situation and need me to come get you."

  You don't have to go over the rules every single time he goes out; just reinforce them occasionally to keep them top of mind.

- **Over an after-school treat.** Create a fun routine, like having a chat over soda or hot chocolate after school, when you talk about any questions or concerns your kid may have around body safety. This could include asking questions like, "How safe do you feel at school?" followed by, "Are there any bullies at your school?" and "Has that kid ever picked on you?"

  To draw your kid out, ask a lot of open-ended questions, which can't be answered with a simple yes or no. If he says someone's picking on him, let him tell you—without interruption—what's been going on. Then ask him how he handled it or would like to handle it. If he needs your guidance, teach him the techniques I shared in Chapter 6 on how to train bullies to leave him alone.

- **When watching movies or TV.** Many of today's movies, TV shows, and video games are fraught with violence and sexual scenes. The characters engage in risky actions, display terrible judgment, make inappropriate sexual comments, behave badly, mistreat others (particularly intimate partners), and make all manner of questionable choices.

Be aware of what your kid is watching and spend time watching with him. Use scenes showing sketchy behavior as opportunities to talk about safety issues, sexual consent, and appropriate behavior.

But rather than lecture him on what not to do, ask his opinion about what he's watching and how *he* would handle such situations. For example:

For scenes showing people engaging in risky behavior (think Johnny Knoxville and friends in *Jackass* doing seriously stupid and potentially deadly pranks for laughs): "Have you ever been in a situation where your friends tried to get you to do something you knew was dangerous? It's really tough to stand up to peer pressure. What could you say to your friends if you didn't want to do something you knew was risky?"

If he shares something alarming that he or his friends have done, try not to freak out; rather, try asking your kid what he learned and gently advise him against taking dares or doing crazy shit to impress others.

For scenes where a character is being abused, or sexual consent is being violated: "Wow. She doesn't look like she's into what he's doing to her. What could you say or do if you found yourself in a situation like that?" Remind him or her that they *always* have the right to say no, to set strong boundaries, and to fight an abuser if it comes down to that.

Badass Grandma's Two Cents

Remember when I told you that the words you say to your child become his inner voice? It's true; you have a place of honor in his noggin that will last throughout his lifetime—whether he likes it or not. Teach him to use that voice when he needs guidance. If he's in a tough spot where his intuition is blaring and he feels frozen with indecision about how to respond, he should ask himself the following: "What would Mom or Dad tell me to do?"

Chances are your kid has a good idea of what you'd advise. The more in tune he is with his intuition, the more quickly he'll recognize and listen to it when he needs to. When it tells him to be careful, to do something differently, he needs to *heed that voice*! It's his best friend and it won't steer him wrong.

Encourage your child to trust his gut and his body and then ACT! If he responds by defending himself from a threatening person—whether it's verbally or physically, or even by just removing himself from the situation—he sends a signal that it's *not* okay for the perpetrator to escalate his behavior. Let your kid know he can be as rude as needed to maintain his boundaries and safety.

CHAPTER 12

Empowering Kids With Disabilities

Why I Wrote This Chapter

As I've spoken around the country about how to protect our kids, I've had a number of parents beg me to include a chapter on how to protect children with disabilities. The first couple of times this happened, I thought it was a good idea but brushed it off because I had no expertise in this area. But after the fifth time a worried mom approached me, I decided I had to find a way to meet the demand for information from these desperate parents.

Then I learned that:

- People (not necessarily just kids) with any kind of physical, mental, developmental, or emotional disability are far more likely to be the victims of sexual assault—up to seven times more likely, according to U.S. Department of Justice data.[167] And this estimate is most likely an undercount because the data didn't count people living in group homes or state institutions and because many victims with disabilities can't communicate what happened to them.[168]

- More than 90 percent of people with intellectual disabilities will experience some form of sexual abuse, and 49 percent will experience 10 or more abusive incidents.[169]

- Nearly 100 percent of predators who abuse people with disabilities are known to the victim.[170] The abusers are often caregivers upon whom the victims are dependent. Research shows that caregivers and developmental disability service providers represent the largest number of identified perpetrators.[171]

- Children with disabilities are two to three times more likely to be bullied than those without disabilities.[172] One study reported that 60 percent of students with disabilities are regularly bullied compared with 25 percent of all students.[173]

Reading this research, I was distraught and horrified. It was clear I had to write about violence against kids living with disabilities in order to give parents the information they need to protect this incredibly vulnerable population.

I'm really not an expert in this area, so I'm bound to make mistakes and say something insensitive or inaccurate at some point in this chapter. Please forgive me when I screw up, and don't send hate mail. Rather, gently correct me so I'll be more aware in the future.

Now, let's get started by being clear on what we're talking about here.

Definitions

Disability: A physical, intellectual, developmental, medical, learning, or other condition that substantially limits one or more major life activity.

Child with a Disability: A child who's been diagnosed with an intellectual disability, hearing impairment, speech or language impairment, visual impairment, serious emotional disturbances, orthopedic impairment, autism, traumatic brain injury, other health impairments, or specific learning disability and who, because of the condition, needs special education and related resources.[174]

Specific Learning Disabilities (SLD): The umbrella term "SLD" covers a specific group of learning challenges that affect a child's ability to read, write, listen, speak, reason, or do math. This includes dyslexia, dysgraphia, auditory processing disorder, and nonverbal learning disabilities. SLD is the most common category used under the Individuals with Disabilities

Education Act, covering about one-third of students who qualified as disabled according to that act.[175]

Physical Disabilities: Conditions that are attributed to a congenital or physical cause that impact mobility and the ability to perform physical activities.

Medical Disabilities: This includes conditions affecting one or more of the body's systems, including the respiratory, immunological, neurological, and circulatory systems.[176] Cancer, lupus, and HIV+/AIDS are included in this category.

Intellectual Disabilities: Kids with this type of disability have below-average intellectual abilities. They may also have poor communication, self-care, and social skills. Down syndrome is one example of an intellectual disability.[177]

Speech and Language Disabilities: Speech and language disabilities may result from hearing loss, cerebral palsy, learning disabilities, and/or physical conditions. These disabilities may range from problems with articulation or voice strength to the complete absence of voice, including difficulties in projection, fluency problems (such as stuttering and stammering), and difficulties articulating particular words or terms.[178]

Learning Disabilities: Learning disabilities are neurologically based and may interfere with learning and listening, speaking, reading, writing, reasoning, or math skills. Kids with learning disabilities may be highly intelligent, but their learning difficulties may lead to poor academic performance.[179]

Developmental Disabilities: These include a diverse group of chronic conditions due to mental or physical impairments that arise before adulthood. Developmental disabilities cause people difficulties in certain areas of life, especially in language, mobility, learning, self-help, and independent living.[180] Some examples of more common developmental disabilities include attention deficit hyperactivity disorder (ADHD), autism spectrum disorders, cerebral palsy, and intellectual disabilities.[181]

Cognitive Disabilities: This category includes limitations in mental functioning and in communication, self-care, and social skills.

Psychiatric Disabilities: These refer to a wide range of behavioral and/ or psychological problems characterized by anxiety, mood swings, depression, or compromised assessment of reality. These behavioral problems persist over time and aren't in response to a particular event.[xxviii][182]

Disability Harassment: This is defined as intimidation or abusive behavior toward a student based on their disability. Harassment of this nature creates a hostile environment by interfering with or denying a student's access to services or opportunities in the institution's program or in receiving benefits due.[183] This can occur in any location connected with the school, including classrooms, cafeterias, hallways, playgrounds, athletic fields, school buses, or during school-sponsored events.[184]

This type of harassment also includes conduct against the family, friends, and associates of a disabled person (such as bullying or hate crimes) because of their connection with that person.

Disability harassment is illegal under Section 504 of the Rehabilitation Act of 1973 and Title II of the Americans with Disabilities Act of 1990.[185]

Individuals with Disabilities Education Act (IDEA): IDEA requires public schools to provide special education and related services to eligible students. Not every child who struggles in school qualifies. To be covered, a child's school performance must be "adversely affected" by a qualified disability.[186]

---

xxviii This definition doesn't include post-traumatic stress disorders, which are related to particular events, but they, too, are considered psychiatric disabilities.

According to Understood.org, the primary aims of IDEA are:[187]

- To provide free, appropriate public education to children with disabilities. IDEA requires schools to identify and evaluate students suspected of having disabilities, at no cost to their families, through a process called Child Find. Once kids are found to have a qualifying disability, schools must provide them with special education and related services (such as speech therapy and counseling) to meet their unique needs and help them make progress in school.

- To give parents (or legal guardians) a voice in their child's education. Under IDEA, you have a say in the decisions the school makes about your child. At every point in the process, the law gives you specific rights and protections called procedural safeguards. For example, one safeguard is that the school must get your consent before providing services to your child.

IDEA covers kids from birth through high school graduation or age 21 (whichever comes first). It provides early intervention services up to age three, and special education for older kids in public schools, including charter schools.

Individualized Education Program (IEP): An IEP is a written statement of the educational program designed to meet a child's individual needs. Every child who receives special education services must have an IEP.[188]

Section 504: Section 504 is an anti-discrimination civil rights statute that requires that the needs of students with disabilities be met in the same way as those of nondisabled students.

How Children Living with Disabilities Learn and Process Information

For any child, grade school is overwhelming and fraught with drama, violence, and murky social swamps. For children living with disabilities, it's all that AND having to manage very real physical, mental, intellectual, or emotional conditions that challenge their ability to perform academically and fit in with their peers.

Children with disabilities learn and process information in unique ways so I won't attempt to generalize here. My purpose in this chapter is to tell you what you need to know to protect your kid with a disability and teach him to protect and defend himself when you're not around—in a way that's appropriate for his developmental and maturity level.

Let's face it, living with a disability puts a big fat target on your child's back that bullies and predators may try to exploit.

My job is to help you turn that target into a shield.

Greatest Threats to These Kids

Please be sure to read each referenced chapter for additional information on the threats and predators your child may encounter. In some places, I've added more information about threats that are pertinent to kids with disabilities.

Bullying

(Refer to Chapter 6)

It's well-known that bullies tend to target kids who are more physically, mentally, socially, or emotionally vulnerable. Children with disabilities make perfect targets not only because they tend to look or act differently than so-called average children, but also because they often can't fight back.

Bullies don't like to be challenged; it threatens the illusion of their authority and makes them look bad (as if picking on a kid in a wheelchair doesn't already make them look like complete tossers!). They choose victims who are unlikely or unable to resist them verbally or physically. And when the victim has a condition that causes him to behave impulsively and reactively, such as ADHD, the bully knows they can easily get a rise out of him and maybe even get *him* in trouble when he acts out in response. Double fun.

Victims may understand that their disability, which they can't control, makes them an easy target, or they may not understand why they're being bullied at all. Some bullies pretend to be nice to their victims to set them up for a fall, and the victims may welcome the attention, believing it's friendly. When/if they discover that the joke's on them, they naturally feel confused, hurt, and betrayed.

What to Teach Your Kid About Bullying

Talking to your child with a disability about bullying from the time he's a tiny tot will prepare him for what he may face as he gets older. Helping him devise a plan now for how to deal with it is really important. Knowing what his options are and that he has a choice about how he responds will give him a sense of control over his own destiny, which is a confidence-builder.

Your kid is going to be teased by other kids at some point, that's pretty much a given. Teach him what bullying behavior looks like and the difference between benign teasing, which is friendly and not meant to be hurtful, and bullying, which *is* meant to be destructive and hurtful.

Say: "Sometimes other kids like to tease each other by saying things like, 'Nice job, Grace,' when you trip, or 'OMG, that was so stupid!' when you say something silly. They might laugh, but they're laughing at what you did, not at you personally. If they tease you, be a good sport and laugh at yourself too. But sometimes there are kids who think it's funny to pick on other kids. They might say something really mean to you or even try to push you around. It's not funny and it isn't okay."

Teach him that bullies like to pick on kids who will either get upset or cry, or who'll get angry and act out, which gets the victim himself in trouble.

If your child has behavioral issues, like ADHD, that cause him to act impulsively, start by saying: "You know how sometimes you like to talk a lot or how you sometimes get worked up when you're upset?"

Or, if he has a condition like autism, say: "You know how you don't like to be touched or have someone get in your space?"

If he has a physical disability, you could say: "There are some kids who like to pick on other kids who use braces/crutches/a wheelchair."

Continue with, "Well, some bullies like to be mean to kids who feel/look like you do. They don't have the courage or inner strength that you do. I'm going to teach you how to use that courage and inner strength to stop bullies." Then teach him the strategies below.

Strategies to Stop Bullying

Help your child come up with several ways he could react to a bully by role-playing different scenarios. Say: "Let's think about different situations when a bully might try to do or say something mean," and then come up with ways he could respond. For example, "What would you do if a bully wouldn't stop picking on you or was making you feel afraid?"

Then let him come up with his own answers. If he falters, prompt him by brainstorming a variety of ways to respond to bullying, such as:

- Avoiding the bully. (You may have to ask the school to move his locker or transfer him to a different class.)
- Ignoring the bully.
- Getting away from the bully, if possible.
- Ask another kid for help by saying, "Go get a teacher."
- Agreeing with the bully. Say, "You're right. I am clumsy sometimes."
- Using humor to defuse the situation. Ask, "Does this wheelchair make my butt look big?"
- Trying sarcasm. Say, "Really? I didn't notice I walk differently."
- Calling the bully on it. Ask, "Why would you say that? That's mean."
- Telling a teacher or other trusted adult (and you) when there's an incident. Help him write a list of who he could tell if someone was bullying him.

When Your Kid's Reaction May Escalate the Bullying or He Initiates It

Bullies love to pick on kids who have disabilities that cause them to behave erratically or act out when provoked because it's "fun" to set them off and get them in trouble. It's not easy to teach a reactive child to regulate his emotions and behavior, but you might be surprised by how far proactive conversations about this topic and role-playing different scenarios can go toward helping him remain more calm and less likely to overreact.

I'm not an expert on exactly how to do this, so I'll leave it to you to research the best ways to help your kid regulate his emotions. What I *can* do is offer some ways you can help him think through his options and re-actions, which will hopefully help during any future incidents.

Ask: "What were you doing just before Josh started bullying you?" And then, "What could you do differently next time so something like this doesn't happen (e.g., avoiding the bully, asking the teacher for help, etc.)?"

Help your child learn to recognize how *his* actions (talking too loudly, acting out, being too affectionate with others) might draw negative attention toward him while at the same time emphasizing that he's not to blame for the bullying; any incidents that occur are the choice and fault of the bully, not his.

Together, make a list of ways your child could change his behavior (e.g., waiting his turn, giving compliments instead of hugs, etc.) and use role-playing scenarios, taking turns being the bully and the victim, to increase his confidence.

If you have a child whose behavior tends to be disruptive, don't automatically assume he started the incident. Kids with behavioral issues can get a bad rep that follows them from teacher to teacher, and they may automatically assume your kid is the cause or equal participant in every incident. Give your child a chance to explain what happened and validate his feelings, if not his reaction to the situation.

If your child *did* start the incident, don't feel like a bad parent and wallow in it. Pour your energy into working with your kid to help him find better ways of interacting with others. Work with the school to come up with consequences that are fair and appropriate for him.

Counseling or behavioral therapy may help him learn to regulate his emotions more effectively, so do consider it. I don't know whether this kind of help is available for free through your child's IEP, but it's worth looking into.

What to Do If Your Child Has Been Bullied

If you learn that your kid's been bullied, it's important to take action to protect him and keep it from happening again. If it happens at school, on the bus, or at a school-sponsored activity, he's protected under IDEA and his school is required to take swift action to ensure he's protected from the bully and given any accommodations he needs to address the problem.

If the abuse is relatively mild, you might try calling the offender's parents to let them know what happened, but only after you've calmed down! If you do call them, don't jump down their throats, and don't talk trash about their kid, which will almost certainly put them on the defensive, even if their "angel" is a total wanker. Instead, dispassionately explain what happened and ask for their help to stop it.

If the bullying escalates beyond taunting and name-calling into the realm of threats of violence or actual violence, go straight to the school principal, superintendent, and/or school board and ask them to investigate the incident and take action to stop the abuse. If they don't do this right away, they may be in violation of state or federal laws.

It'll be helpful if you prepare a written timeline of the incident(s), explaining the facts as you know them, including who was involved and witnessed the incident; when it happened; what occurred before, during, and after the incident; where it happened; why it happened; and how it happened.

And this is important: Keep detailed records of all communications you have with school officials, teachers, guidance counselors, etc., including who you talked to, when you talked to them, what was said and promised, and what was actually done. Ask them to tell you when action is taken. While the school may not be able to tell you what sanctions it imposed against the bully, they do have to tell you what changes are being implemented to protect your child.

If the school doesn't address the problem and protect your kid, you can file a formal complaint with the U.S. Department of Education's Office for Civil Rights.[xxix] Know that you MUST file your complaint within 180 days of the incident! If that deadline has passed and/or you feel your child is being denied free appropriate public education in violation of the Americans with Disability Act, you can file a request for an impartial hearing with your state's Department of Education within two years of the incident.

You can also get legal advice from an attorney who specializes in disability harassment cases. Legal action isn't usually necessary; just the threat is often enough to spur a school system into action. Bullying isn't yet illegal in the U.S., but bullying or harassing a child with a disability *IS*.

Working with Your Child's School and Teachers

If you're concerned that your child is at risk of being bullied, talk to her school's administrators and teachers to implement activities that encourage peer relationships and help cultivate empathy.

A few strategies to try, published by StopItNow.org:[189]

- Have students come up with fun activities that include everyone in the class or school. For example, some schools have students with disabilities and nondisabled students eat lunch together. This ensures that no one feels left out or isolated.

- Teach nondisabled students upfront about the kind of support their peers with disabilities need.

- Create a buddy system for kids with disabilities.

- Help students come up with strategies to adapt the classroom so it meets the needs of children with disabilities.

- Conduct team-based learning activities and rotate student groups so all students get to interact. One school requires its clubs to rotate leadership roles, ensuring every member gets a chance to run the group.

- Reward positive, helpful, inclusive behavior.

---

xxix Go to www.ed.gov/about/offices/list/ocr/complaintprocess.html

Tell your child's school officials and teachers that you'll be closely monitoring things because of the increased risk she faces, and that you want to be notified immediately if there are any incidents involving her. Also request a special IEP or Section 504 meeting when you ask to have anti-bullying and social skills training added to her program.

Teach Your Child How to Make and Keep Friends

In Chapter 13, I'll help you teach your child how to make friends and be a good friend. Check it out!

Online Dangers

(Refer to Chapter 7)

The internet and social media can help your kid be more social and independent, but they also put her at greater risk of being cyberbullied. Kids who would never dream of physically bullying a child with a disability could become her tormentors online when disinhibited by the anonymity the internet provides.

Even peers who are sympathetic to your child may go along with the crowd and say hateful things to or about her in order to fit in. They might feel terrible when they do this, but not nearly as bad as your kid feels when people she thought were her friends suddenly troll her online.

Pornography

(Refer to Chapter 7 on Online Dangers)

Molestation and Sexual Assault

(Refer to Chapter 8)

Everything I wrote in Chapter 8 on child sexual molestation and sexual assault applies to your child with a disability, so I won't repeat it here. But I would like to take a minute to address the importance of teaching your child with a disability about sex and human sexuality (in an age-appropriate way, of course) to protect her from abuse and assault.

Many people never consider that people with disabilities, including severe physical disabilities, desire love and intimacy like everyone else. Your tween or teen who lives with a disability is a sexual being and, like any kid, will have sexual thoughts and desires as he grows older.

Because children with disabilities are at an increased risk of being sexually abused, it's imperative that you talk to your kid about sex and safe versus unsafe touch—at her maturity and developmental level, of course.[xxx]

According to StopItNow.org, "All children, even those with severe disabilities, need to understand basic concepts like the differences between boys and girls, accurate names for all body parts, and where babies come from.

"When you present this information in a matter-of-fact way, your kid learns that it's okay to come to you with questions or concerns. Adapt how you present this information to your child by using tools, including role-playing, structured play with dolls, books, and videos, etc."[190]

Your kid needs you to prepare her for the physical changes he'll experience during puberty. If you're unsure when your child might start to experience these changes, talk to his pediatrician.

According to a 2013 report,[191] one of the main reasons kids with disabilities are at an elevated risk of sexual assault is their lack of basic knowledge about sexual health and relationships.

The report states: "This practice can be traced to a desire to shield children with disabilities from the realities of life as well as a belief *that people with disabilities are asexual.* (Italics are mine.) As a result, sexual education is rarely provided in special education classrooms and, when it is, it's not tailored to the needs of children with disabilities".

"Moreover, family members may have personal anxieties about their children having sex and, therefore, will not raise these issues with them or

---

xxx StopItNow.org has a whole library of incredible tip sheets on how to protect children from sexual abuse and teach them healthy behaviors. It even has one specifically on the sexual development of children with disabilities, which I reference in the Resources section of my website at www.cjscarlet.com/resources.

the schools. As such, children with disabilities are not taught about their bodies, don't learn to distinguish between good touch and bad touch, and are never given a framework for what constitutes a healthy relationship. Without such fundamental lessons, children with disabilities have no language to describe what has happened to them when they are abused."[192]

Teaching your kid about body safety, sexual health, and healthy relationships is such an easy and effective way to protect her from predators.

So do it.

Talk to Your Kid's Caregivers

Your child's caregivers may be her greatest threat. Make sure you're 100 percent comfortable with them and that your intuition gives you a thumbs-up. Vet them thoroughly and then make them your allies by talking to them about your family rules regarding privacy and safe touch. Ask for their feedback on areas of concern regarding your child and get their input on how best to safeguard her.

As I mentioned in the introduction to this chapter, children with disabilities are most often abused or assaulted by the people who take care of them (family members and paid caregivers). Teach your child from the time she's little how to identify when something inappropriate is happening, how to say no to caregivers and others, and that she should always tell you if something or someone makes her feel uncomfortable, scared, or violated.

Refer to StopItNow.org's website for more great information on how to address sexuality and sexual abuse involving children with disabilities. The site also has a tip sheet called *How to Protect Your Child from Sexual Abuse in Program Settings*.[193]

Discussing Body Safety

We've established the importance of teaching your child with a disability about body safety issues, including sex and human sexuality. You know your kid better than anyone else and only you can decide when your child is ready to learn these important facts. My advice is to start as soon as you think he has the ability to understand what you're saying.

Remember, this isn't about having one extended safety talk with your child where you tell him everything there is to know about danger and walk away thinking you've done your job and now he's safe. Rather, you'll want to introduce body safety topics in tiny doses over time throughout his life.

Approach the subject of body safety matter-of-factly: Say, "It's time we went over the rules about body safety" or "I want to have a talk today about body safety."

You can stop at any point if you think he can't understand you or is getting overwhelmed. You can always try again when he's a little older.

Don't worry if you don't say it perfectly or get flustered; you're going to make this part of your routine and you'll get better at it over time. In Chapter 15, I'll help you learn how to incorporate safety talks into your daily conversations and the monthly family meetings I recommend. The point of making it an ongoing conversation early on is to have it become a habit for you and your child that will still work even when he's a rebellious teenager.

When to Teach Your Kid About Body Safety Issues

If you want your kid to pay attention when you talk about body safety issues, choose a time when you're both comfortable and relaxed. Try to time it so that neither of you are stressed or cranky.

Consider the following times to have body safety conversations with your child:

- **While changing clothes.** When your child is changing clothes, make it a habit to say something like, "Time to cover up! Your private parts are just for you, right? Remember, no one else should look or touch your privates except [Mom/Dad/caregiver, etc.] when you need to get clean, or the doctor when you need help to stay healthy."

- **Bath time.** This is a great time to talk to your child about his body parts, using the correct terminology.

- **Movie time.** When you watch movies with your kid, talk about them afterward, highlighting any moral lessons and safety themes (e.g., the debatable wisdom of the main character walking down that dark alley alone). Ask open-ended questions like, "What should you do if that happened to you?" and use your child's answer for further discussion. Keep it light. (I do NOT recommend talking about danger topics just before bed.)

- **Over a snack.** Create a fun routine, like having a chat over hot cocoa or milk and cookies, when you talk about any questions or concerns he may have around body safety. This could include asking questions like, "How safe do you feel at school?" followed by, "Are there any bullies at your school?" and "Has that kid ever picked on you?" Use his answers to talk in greater depth about how he or you) should handle any threatening situations.

- **Before any new situation.** Before your kid interacts with new people, talk to him about what he might experience and who he might meet. Make it a fun conversation by talking about what adventures he'll have. Reiterate the most important body safety issues, such as trusting his intuition and saying no to hugs, then ask if he has any questions.

What to Teach Your Child

Boundaries

Kids with disabilities are often "manhandled" by caregivers who need to dress, bathe, change, or move them. So, it's important that your child learns to have good physical and emotional boundaries and to recognize if they're violated.

You should always ask permission before touching your child and tell her what you're about to do (dress or bathe her, for example). If it's something you have to do regardless of her wishes, say this instead: "I'm going to give you a bath now," rather than asking for permission. Ask your child's other caregivers to be sure to respect her boundaries.

Saying No

Teach your child with a verbal disability a variety of ways she can say no that don't require verbal skills. These can include shaking her head, stomping her feet, flailing her arms, or slapping the offender to get him to stop.

Safe vs. Unsafe Touch

This can be a tough concept to grasp depending on the type of disability your child has and the degree to which she needs help from caregivers. If she needs help with things like bathing or going to the bathroom, explain to her that it's okay for her caregivers to undress her or pull down her pants, wash or wipe her private parts, and help her get dressed again. Tell her it's *not* okay for them to touch her private parts outside of this (unless there are other intimate functions she needs help with that I'm not familiar with) or to touch her in any way that makes her feel uncomfortable, scared, or confused.

Talk to caregivers about ways to effectively care for your child while meeting her needs for privacy and appropriate touch. Agree on ways to make her less vulnerable to harm or abuse.

Sharing your family rules on boundaries, privacy, and safe touch will help guide the caregivers' efforts to provide only the level of personal care she requires. It also puts them on notice that you're a watchful, protective parent whose kid is not to be messed with!

Safe vs. Unsafe People

I mentioned this before but want to reiterate it as a great conversation starter: Draw a circle and put the names of your child's safe people inside the circle. Then ask her to name the "unsafe" people she wants to put outside the circle. Gently and carefully ask her about each person she put outside the circle to find out why she doesn't trust them and considers them unsafe. Pay close attention to clues as to why these people may pose a threat to her.

Let the people you and your child identify as "safe" know they've been chosen and that your child may want to come to them to talk about body safety issues or concerns. Make sure they're okay with being on the list.

Share this chapter with them so they can educate themselves and be ready and able to spot potential concerns they should bring to your attention.

Telling

Kids with disabilities are not only less likely to disclose abuse, they're less likely to be taken seriously when they do. Some reasons your child might not disclose abuse include:

- A physical or intellectual limitation that inhibits her ability to tell
- The belief she brought it on herself or feelings of unworthiness because of her disability
- Feeling powerless to stop the abuse
- Not wanting to alienate the abuser or get him in trouble
- Being afraid she won't find another "friend"
- Feeling dependent on the abuser for her welfare
- Feelings of love or admiration for the abuser

Reassure your child that it's okay and important to tell you if anything inappropriate, scary, or confusing happens to her.

If You Have Concerns That Your Child Has Been Victimized

I cover this topic very thoroughly in the chapters on Bullying, Online Dangers, and Sexual Molestations and Assault, so refer to these for detailed information on what to do if you suspect or learn your child has been victimized.

Badass Grandma's Two Cents

Let your child know often that you support her. Tell her you'll always love her no matter what, even if she tells you something scary or bad. Let her know you've got her back and will always do your very best to protect her from harm. Just as important, tell her you'll help her learn to protect and defend *herself* so she can feel more confident and in charge of herself and her life.

PART IV

Taking Your Kid to the Next Level

In this section, I talk about how to give your child confidence and build her self-esteem, so sketchy people know she's not to be messed with. I also share my "rabid Tasmanian devil," moves she can use to defend herself physically if an attack is imminent. Finally, I'll tell you how to use regular family meetings to introduce body safety topics and build stronger bonds with your kid.

CHAPTER 13

Confidence Rules!

"Everyone is a genius. But if you judge a fish by its ability to climb a tree, it will live its whole life believing that it is stupid."

Author Unknown (And no, it WASN'T Einstein)

Like Bear Repellant, Only Better

Do you know the number one predator repellant? *Confidence!* Kids (and adults) who are confident and self-assured are less likely to be targeted by predators. You see, perps like to target people with low self-esteem because they're more vulnerable and less likely to resist or tell.

Kids with confidence are social magnets. Because they feel good about themselves, they assume other kids will like them and want to play with them. Confidence is a very attractive energy. Desperation, on the other hand, is a stinky cologne that other kids and predators can smell a mile away.

I know how heartbreaking it is to worry about your kid when she's shy or socially awkward. When my son was around seven, he was struggling socially after skipping a grade. I wanted him to be tough and be able to roll with the punches, but I also wanted to nurture his sensitivity and compassion. Mostly I didn't want him to be a target for bullies.

As a single mom, I had no idea how to raise him to be a strong yet sensitive young man who fit in with his peers. It was agonizing. After many fits and starts, he eventually found his way. Now he's the father of three, including one boy, and he'll have to deal with the same issues.

And *that's* why I wrote this chapter. I hope to spare you the agony of watching helplessly while your child flails socially or suffers the pain of not having friends or not being accepted by other kids. This chapter is all about how to instill confidence and self-esteem in your kid, which can be life-altering for her.

What Confidence and Self-Esteem Look Like

Confidence and self-esteem go hand in hand; it's nearly impossible, really, to have one without the other. Confidence is the feeling of self-assuredness that comes from appreciating your own qualities, abilities, and even limitations.

People with a healthy sense of self-esteem project confidence and self-respect, and they expect (and generally receive) the respect of others. And it pays off, literally. Studies have proven that teenagers and young adults with high levels of confidence outearn their less confident peers later in life.

Confident people unconsciously ward off predators. They carry themselves differently (heads up, eyes clear), and their energy projects power and purpose. They may be victimized in one-off incidents, but they are the least likely to be targeted by criminals.

Here's what a child who's confident and has high self-esteem looks like:

- She has a positive outlook on life.
- She doesn't wallow in negative self-talk. She's able to meet new people and quickly make friends.
- She doesn't have a victim mentality, meaning she doesn't feel like life is happening *to* her or is outside her control.
- She doesn't beat herself up over her "weaknesses," focusing more on her strengths.
- She has strong boundaries and the willingness to enforce them.
- She doesn't feel compelled to go along with the crowd or popular opinion.
- She can say no to her peers and even adults when necessary.

- She can accept *constructive* criticism.
- She takes responsibility for her choices.
- She doesn't take things personally and/or is able to quickly move past personal slights and disappointments.

Youngsters are naturally confident, and their self-esteem is off the charts. They're like puppy dogs who eagerly bounce back after every scolding— unless their spirits are warped over time by dysfunctional family dynamics or verbal, physical, or sexual abuse.

However, as they get close to puberty, many kids (especially girls) seem to fall off a cliff and their self-esteem plummets. They begin to compare themselves and their bodies (and their houses and clothes and parents— you get the picture) to their peers and usually find themselves coming up short in their own minds.

Of course, some kids are naturally shy and anxious for no discernable reason. Every child's personality is unique and should be celebrated, but, with enough patience and loving guidance, the above qualities can be nurtured in your kid and can enable her to face the world more confidently.

What a Lack of Confidence and Self-Esteem Look Like

The cost of *not* fostering your child's confidence and self-esteem is incredibly high. Without healthy amounts of both, he's more vulnerable to bullies and other predators and more likely to be targeted by them.

Here's what a child with low levels of confidence and self-esteem looks like:

- He feels unworthy of respect or positive treatment.
- He engages in negative self-talk and destructive behaviors.
- He feels anxious or depressed.
- He withdraws from peers and social situations.
- He shies away from new experiences.
- He has few or no friends.

- He expects people to treat him badly, and passively accepts it.
- He puts the needs and wants of others ahead of his own.
- He seeks negative attention (meaning he acts out to get attention because he doesn't feel he can get it through positive behavior).
- He resists positive interactions and people.
- He doesn't set boundaries and feels unable to stand up for himself.
- He takes responsibility for other people's feelings and problems.
- He trusts no one or naïvely trusts everyone.
- He's acutely sensitive to criticism and slights from others.
- He lacks the ability to bounce back from disappointment or trauma.

This is such a sad list, and I know way too many kids and adults who carry these tragic characteristics on their weary backs. Of course, kids can—and often do—have traits from both categories. Every child is unique and special and that's okay. Just know that you have the power to help your child transform his negative traits into more positive attitudes and behaviors.

Let's talk about how to do that.

How to Raise a Confident Kid with Healthy Self-Esteem

I remember one time when my younger son, then about 12, seemed really glum. When I asked him what was going on, he finally told me that he thought he was ugly. I had to bite my tongue to keep from brushing off his concerns and telling him he was actually quite handsome, which he was (and still is).

Here's what I said instead: "Do you remember the reason you chose Tiger [your cat]?"

My son laughed, "Yeah, he was the most wild and playful one, and he bit me."

"That's right," I said. "You picked Tiger because his personality was different from all the other cats. You didn't want just some ordinary old cat.

And do you remember that you also thought his face was really funny?" My son nodded.

"Well, that cute, funny face of his and his wild personality are exactly what make you love him, right?" He nodded again thoughtfully.

I looked at my son deeply, projecting all the love I felt for him from my eyes, and said, "You're cute and funny and you're wild, and *that's* what people love about you! Don't ever change a thing."

My son smiled and said, "Thanks, Mom," and went into his room.

I tell you this story to point out that many, if not most, kids go through a period thinking they're ugly or stupid or socially inept. And it may be true that they're less attractive, less smart, or less socially "ept" than the average bear. If your child feels this way, it's your job, Mom and Dad, to help him reframe his perspective to better appreciate his uniqueness.

Your Child's Social Reinvention Plan

Reassure your ugly duckling that she'll one day be a social swan and that you'll work with her to come up with a plan to help her do that. Here are some strategies you can use:

- Encourage her to take pride in her personal appearance by helping her maintain good personal hygiene. Tell her that others like people who look and smell clean and healthy. Show her how to properly brush her teeth and fix her hair, have her bathe and wash her hair regularly (showing her how to completely shampoo and rinse!), and do your best to dress her like her peers (even thrift stores often have contemporary clothes in stock). Kids who are smelly and dress differently from everyone else are candidates for bullying.

- Teach her about sex and human sexuality so she becomes familiar with her body's functions and more comfortable in her own skin. Knowing what to expect in terms of physical changes as she approaches and deals with puberty will keep her from feeling shocked or ashamed when she's taken over by the invasion of the body snatchers.

- Encourage her to pursue activities she really enjoys and is good at so she'll feel more confident about her abilities and what she has to offer the world. At the same time, help her identify areas where she could use improvement (e.g., seeing a dermatologist to control her acne or getting a tutor so she can keep up in class). If she comes up with things that can't be "fixed" (like ditching her braces), work with her to alter her attitude about them. Just about anything can be turned into a positive if you think about it the right way.

- Show her the life-changing magic of helping others whenever she can through both random acts of kindness and regular volunteer efforts (preferably with you by her side, modeling good behavior). I can't say enough about the power of generosity. Helping others in need connects your child to humanity and opens her heart to the suffering of others, which helps her develop empathy and compassion and teaches her to appreciate her own good fortune.

- Talk to her about self-respect and advise her not to accept disrespectful behavior from others. Teach her that respect works both ways and that to gain respect, she must first offer it.

- Show her (through your example) how to stand up for the rights and protection of others. That means speaking up to express her disapproval of racist, sexist, or any other "ist" jokes or behavior. The offender may get his feelings hurt, but others will have greater respect for her for standing up to others' inappropriate remarks.

- Help her learn how to make friends and be a good friend. (I cover this below.)

- Tell her that she always has a choice about how she responds to the slings and arrows of life, including others' words and behavior. Remind her often that life isn't about what happens to her, but how she *deals with what happens to her.*

- Reassure her that it's okay to laugh at herself. The best way to teach this is to laugh at *yourself!* Point out that often the most embarrassing things become the funniest stories she'll tell years later.

- Help her gain new skills and learn about responsibility by giving her chores to do around the house. Give her an allowance (however small; it could even be computer or TV time) to increase her confidence and help her develop a solid work ethic. This will also give her a small income (or that coveted computer or gaming time), which will enhance her feeling of independence.

- Tell her to expect that when she tries a new activity or project, she's probably going to suck at it at first. Remind her that everyone's a beginner when they try something new, and they also feel awkward and uncomfortable and worry about looking stupid. Reassure her that she'll get better with practice and perseverance.

- Assure her that it's okay to fail; in fact, it's inevitable if she's trying new things and taking healthy risks.

- Help her to become more resilient. I learned how to do this by watching my son and daughter-in-law with their children. Rather than rushing in to pick them up every time they fall or fail, they reassure their kids that they're okay and to try again.

- Teach her how to sincerely apologize by looking the other person (kid or adult) in the eyes and saying: "I'm really sorry." Short, sweet, and effective. Tell her that apologizing resolves most situations and makes people want to forgive her.

- Assure her that you'll love her no matter where she falls on the gender and sexual orientation map. Let her dress like Batman for Halloween or, as my grandson did when he was two, let him dance with abandon in his sister's Belle costume to the tune of "Let It Go."[xxxi]

- Show her how to make comfortable eye contact with others (not staring them down, remembering to blink, not shifting her eyes back and forth or to the sides). Also teach her how to properly shake hands with a firm yet easy grip.

- Show her how to walk (or roll) like a badass. Together, read a book on body language and talk about how she can carry herself more con-

---

xxxi Yes, I know "Let It Go" is from *Frozen* and not *Beauty and the Beast*. My grandson didn't care; he just danced!

fidently. Have her notice the way other people carry themselves and have her guess what their body language is saying.

- Absolutely teach her to use her growing badass bod to protect herself from danger by demonstrating how to use the Taz moves I offer in the next chapter and have her practice them until she gets the hang of it. Just knowing that she's able to protect herself will increase her confidence right there!

A Note about Teaching These Lessons to Children with Disabilities

I recognize that children with disabilities may have a tougher time learning or living these ideas. If your tween or teen has a disabling condition that leads him to be more impulsive or that affects his physical appearance, he may feel especially ashamed of himself. Try the strategies I mention in the Social Reinvention Plan list above to help him find his social footing.

One helpful idea is for you both to watch online videos about kids with disabilities doing cool things. Some deliver speeches internationally, others climb mountains even though they're blind. Your kid doesn't have to conquer the world or become a daredevil, but I guarantee the perseverance and positivity of these high-achieving kids will inspire him.

How to Make and Keep Friends

It never occurs to most parents that they need to teach their kids how to make and keep friends, but you'd be surprised at the number of children who don't have a clue how to comfortably do this. That said, it's up to you to impress upon your child that knowing how to make and foster friendships is an important life skill.

Making New Friends

If your kid struggles to make friends, before he goes on his next social outing or to a new school or grade level, come up with a plan for how he might approach other kids.

If he's an introvert or awkward in social situations, say: "This evening we're going to the Johnsons' Super Bowl party and there are going to be lots of other kids there. Let's talk about how you can make friends while we're there so you have someone to hang out with."

Expect that your shy or nervous child may not be enthusiastic about the idea at this point. Nevertheless, you should continue. Say, "You can go up to another kid or group of kids and introduce yourself. Then ask if you can join the conversation. It's as easy as that!" Then continue, "If they say no, you can say, 'Okay. Maybe later,' and go up to a different kid or group."

Most kids will happily let a newbie into the circle, but let's face it, tweens and teens can be cliquish and cruel sometimes, so let your kid know that if he's rejected, it's probably not his fault. In truth, he doesn't want to hang out with any kids who act like that anyway. Encourage him to keep trying to meet new people until he finds his "tribe."

Note: If other kids refuse to hang out with your kid, there might be a reason. If so, you need to find out what it is and then address the problem. Do his clothes smell like cat pee? Is he a bully? Is he socially inept and awkward to be around? Does he have an unfair reputation because he threw up in gym class that one time back in fifth grade?

You can do a lot to fix this. Wash his clothes, teach him how to be kind and friendly, get help to improve his social skills, help him learn to shrug off peer criticism and teasing, and implement the Social Reinvention Plan. Parent up and help your kid find his footing.

Being a Good Friend

Next, teach your child how to have an actual conversation. Say: "When you're trying to make a new friend, it helps to ask them about themselves. You could say something like, 'I really like your Imagine Dragons t-shirt. Have you ever been to one of their concerts?'" Teaching your kid to ask open-ended questions that can't be answered by a monosyllabic yes or no will draw the other kid out.

It can be tricky teaching this because kids sometimes tend to blurt out too much information, which can shock or intimidate others. Inform him that sharing too much personal information too soon can be a turnoff and make things awkward.[xxxii]

Teach him to introduce new facts about himself slowly, over time, following the lead of the other person: Your kid gives his name, and the other kid gives hers. He says he goes to Millbrook Middle School, and she tells him she goes to Kennedy. He shares his favorite subject, and she does the same. It's much like a tennis match in which the two play off each other.

Teach your child how to compliment others by looking for things he actually likes about the other kid. (Advise him to look for neat things about their personality or abilities, rather than their appearance, and tell him not to fake it; kids can spot a phony.)

Say: "People like it when others notice good things about them. If you like the way another kid runs super-fast or throws a football, you could say, 'Wow! That's really cool! Could you teach me how to do that?'"

Teach him how to end their time together by thanking the other kid. Tell him, "When you're done talking or playing with someone, you can say, 'That was really fun. Thanks.'" Even older kids like being appreciated and will remember your child for making them feel good.

Badass Grandma's Two Cents

You have the ability to help your kid actualize his full potential in all areas of his life—social, emotional, and psychological. Even if they pretend to ignore you most of the time, your kid looks to you for guidance about how to be a decent and functional human being.

For those of you who were raised by loving, attentive parents who knew what they were doing, you have great role models to follow. For those who were raised by wolves, well, you have to figure it out as you go along. If you feel confident that you know how to do that, outstanding! If not, read parenting books or ask the awesome parents you know how to teach your child what you yourself weren't taught when you were young.

---

xxxii Hell, I do this ALL the time; a lot of adults do. Telling your kid that might help him feel less like a dork when he does it himself.

Knowing that you don't have all the answers is half the battle; the other half is being willing to keep searching until you find those answers and then apply them.

You've got this!

CHAPTER 14

Teaching Your Kid to Fight Like Taz

Your Kid Has More Power Than Either of You Realize!

Think your kid can't protect herself because she's not a martial artist? Hasn't taken formal self-defense classes? Because she's too young? Physically disabled? Too timid?

Remember when your kid was little and you tried to drag her squirming body to bed? When her tiny little body went limp and she did that frustrating slinky thing, she might as well have weighed a thousand pounds. Trying to maneuver a resistant kid is almost impossible. Your older child can use that same trick with a predator who's trying to molest or abduct her.

You'd be surprised at how much damage your darling can do when she's motivated by fear and anger. I like to teach kids and adults how to fight by having them channel their "inner rabid Tasmanian devil," or "Taz" for short.

The Australian Tasmanian devil, although the size of a small dog, has the strongest bite of any land mammal and is so ferocious it can repel almost any predator that comes its way. "Taz" is a whirlwind of fists, feet, fangs, and raw power. In addition, the real Tasmanian devil uses a pungent body odor and nerve-racking screech to ward off its enemies.

Your child also has powerful weapons at her disposal in the event of an attack, and they're all contained within her own body.

Using Your Kid's Badass Bod to Protect Herself

Fear is our friend because it tells us when we're in danger. Fear isn't to be squelched; it's to be used as rocket fuel to propel your child into action to save her butt from harm.

Say: "If you follow our family rules, you should be safe. But if anyone ever tries to hurt you or take you away, or if they try to do something inappropriate to you and you can't run away, you can always try to fight them off. You know who 'Taz' is, right?" (Explain, if necessary, that he's the "Tasmanian devil" cartoon character. Go so far as to look up a YouTube video of one of the Taz cartoons on the web to show your kid how he spins and wreaks havoc.) Then continue, "Well, I'm going to teach you to fight just like Taz so you can get away from dangerous people."

After you've taught her the Taz techniques I cover below, make her show you how she'd fight and yell, using a pillow or couch cushion she can hit and kick. Gently correct her form or encourage her to yell more loudly as needed to help her get it down pat.

You need to let your child know that if she has to fight off an attacker or would-be kidnapper, she has your permission to do so with as much ferocity and ruthlessness as she can muster. Encourage her to fight as dirty and unfairly as she can, going for the predator's weakest spots—the groin, nose, and throat, and anywhere else on their body she can kick, grab, bite, or twist.

Say: "I give you my permission to be just as wild as you can get, and fight as hard and meanly as you can to get away from bad people, even if it means hurting them."

Your kid gives herself the best chance of getting away and finding help by yelling at the top of her lungs and biting, clawing, kicking, gouging, pinching, twisting, and punching every vulnerable point she can reach on the perpetrator's body.

If she's confronted by an attacker, tell her to get angry! Tell her to get *FURIOUS!* After all, this person is trying to hurt her! Tell her to do whatever it takes to stop the creep who's trying to hurt her. She doesn't owe it to them to be nice or polite. Again, give her permission to unleash her "inner Taz" and fight as dirty as she possibly can until she can get away or the perpetrator flees.

Predators are incredible cowards; they choose victims based on their ability to control them. If your child goes off like a rabid animal the minute someone starts to mess with her, she'll make predators think twice before targeting her.

Now, having said all this, you also need to warn your kid not to use these fighting skills to resolve spats with friends or siblings, or even run-of-the-mill bullies; they're to be reserved for when she's in actual danger of bodily harm or sexual assault.

Martial Arts and Self-Defense Classes—Yes or No?

I highly recommend enrolling your kid in martial arts or self-defense courses *in addition to* teaching him the Taz moves below. All these will increase your child's self-confidence and help him be better prepared to fight back against predators.

But I have one caveat: Don't think that having your kid take a few karate or self-defense classes is going to cut it. In fact, taking just one or a handful of classes could give him a false sense of security. For the training to stick in your child's mind and muscle memory, he must master the techniques, and that requires years of practice. Again, I think this training is a great idea when your eye is on long-term mastery.

It's Go Time!

Teach your child that if a predator tries to physically or sexually assault him, he should start yelling as loudly as he can (yelling is more powerful than screaming, and it'll help him breathe and make him sound more powerful).

Loudly yelling, "NO! Get away from me!" prepares his mind to defend his body, can summon attention and help, and will let the predator know he's not going to be an easy target.

If yelling doesn't send the perpetrator running or your kid can't get away and has to defend himself, teach him to fight like Taz for all he's worth, using the techniques I share below.

Your Kid's Badass Body's Arsenal

Teach your child the following techniques, being sure to role-play and practice them (using a couch cushion or pillow and being careful not to actually hurt you or him):

- **Voice:** Tell your kid that his voice is one of the most powerful tools in his self-defense arsenal. While he's fighting, he should continue to yell as loudly as he can to both bring attention to the situation and to scare the perp into running away.

- **Eyes:** If he's in a furious fight for his life with a predator, tell him to go for the perp's eyes with his fingers. He should press his fingers or thumbs as hard as he can into the inside corners of the person's eyes until the perpetrator backs off, hopefully giving your kid time to run away.

- **Head:** Whether he's being held from the front or behind, your child can swing his head forward or backward into the predator's face or head. I don't recommend attempting to head-butt the offender with his forehead. This may look cool in the movies, but the forehead is actually a fairly sensitive area. Tell him to use the top or back of his skull to connect with the perp's face.

- **Teeth:** Your kid can chomp down on any body part that comes close to his face. It doesn't matter where he bites the offender, it's going to hurt so badly the person will howl with pain. With luck, the attacker will stop whatever he's doing, giving your kid precious time to get into a better fighting position or run away.

- **Palm:** He can use the butt of his open palm to thrust upward toward the attacker's chin or nose. A good uppercut with the butt of his hand can snap the perpetrator's head back and make his eyes water, giving your kid a chance to run away.

- **Fist:** His closed fist can be used to pound on the attacker like a hammer. (Show him how to keep his thumbs on the outside of his fists so he doesn't break his fingers.)

- **Fingers:** Pinching and twisting the predator's skin is incredibly painful. Tell him to grab the attacker's skin and twist as hard as he can and to not let go until the person backs off. He can also use his fingernails to gouge and scratch the attacker's eyes and skin.

- **Elbows:** Your child can slam his elbows into the predator's chest, stomach, face, or head (anywhere, really).

- **Arms:** Your kid can also grab onto something stable—a pole, a tree, his bike—and refuse to let go, screaming at the top of his lungs: "Stop! Help! He's trying to attack/kidnap me!" until the perp gives up and runs for it.

- **Knees:** He can use his knees to kick the perpetrator in the groin when he's in close range or smash it into his nose when he's bent over. He should keep kneeing the attacker until he falls to the ground so your child can get away.

- **Feet:** Your kid's feet can be dangerous when he swipes, stomps, and kicks any of the predator's body parts as violently as he can manage.

- **Whole body:** Your child can rotate his arms really fast in a big circle, like a windmill, to keep the predator from getting close enough to grab him. Remind him to keep yelling for help while he's using his body to fight the attacker off.

Again, I go back to the image of the cartoon Taz who is literally a tornado of fury and might. Your kid's battle with a predator doesn't have to win points for form or style; tell him to just go completely bonkers and he'll take the attacker by surprise and rattle him, hopefully making him flee the scene in fear for his own life!

Tell him not to stop until:

- The predator stops his attack.
- The predator flees the scene.
- He's disabled the predator enough that they can't follow him if he runs away.
- Help arrives and he's safe from the predator.

Work with your kid to practice these moves over and over until he feels comfortable and able to do them. The monthly family meetings I suggest in the next chapter would be the perfect time for practice sessions.

Remember, you're showing your kid how to do these moves as you talk about them, starting by doing them in slow motion. Then have him duplicate these moves using a pillow or couch cushion—NOT an actual person. (I have several videos on my website that show you some of these techniques. You can find them on my video blog at www.cjscarlet.com/vlog.)

Many of these moves can be done by kids with disabilities too, so don't think your child is defenseless just because he's in a wheelchair or uses braces. Of course, you want to be sensitive to his maturity and developmental level when you broach this subject, but DO teach him how to defend himself to the best of his ability.

Remember, your kid has more power than either you or he may think, and he can exercise that power to escape dangerous situations. So, encourage him to let loose his inner Taz!

Badass Grandma's Two Cents

Your kid needs to understand that if someone tries to hurt her, she needs to do everything in her power to protect herself.

She must assume she's fighting for her life, ESPECIALLY if the perp threatens her with a weapon or tries to force her into going with him to another location (where she'll almost certainly be in grave danger of harm). Your child's chances of being shot or stabbed by the offender at the original location are smaller than the chance she'll be seriously injured or killed if she goes with him.

Look, I know you don't want to scare the hell out of your kid, but you need to let her know what she's up against.

And remember to emphasize—and RE-EMPHASIZE—that *the Taz moves are for self-defense in actual emergencies only* and are not to be used against siblings or friends during fights or play.

CHAPTER 15

Keep the Conversation Going

I've said it several times—confidence is the number one predator repellant. And where does a kid's confidence come from? YOU, his parents—through your positive attention and ongoing communications that let your kid know he's loved and cared for.

Of course, parents are constantly paying attention to their children, but how much of that is mindful, purposeful attention versus just reacting to what their kids are doing at any given moment? For "attention" to count, both parent and child must be emotionally and mentally *present* and focused on each other.

Two great ways to make this a habit are to conduct daily check-ins with your tween or teen, which keep you up to date on the issues he's dealing with, and family meetings, which provide prime opportunities to talk about body safety issues and make important family decisions.

Daily Sharing

Everyone likes to do a data dump at the end of the day. A good venting, as long as it doesn't devolve into an angry rant that contaminates the person listening, is healthy and enables you to release the cares of your day and start your family time with greater energy and patience. Kids are no different.

The daily check-in is a conversation you have with your tween or teen as you're driving him home from school or soccer practice, or as you're fixing dinner (you can do it any time, really, although I don't recommend doing it right before you put him to bed unless you want him lying awake for the next hour pondering his day).

Making it a daily ritual helps you stay on top of what's going on with your kid and shows him you're paying attention and are interested in his perspective on life—major confidence boosters.

Asking Questions

If you merely ask, "How was your day, hon?" while you're thumbing through your phone, you're going to get a quiet, "Fine" and that's about it. C'mon, man! You can do better than that! And so can your kid. His day wasn't "fine;" it was filled with laughter and frustration and wonder, and all kinds of epic fails.

Asking your kid open-ended questions will ensure you get more than simple yes or no answers and will create a stronger connection between you. Below are my favorite questions to ask kids:

- Did anything really funny happen today?
- Did you help someone else today? What did you do? How did that make you feel?
- Did anyone get in trouble today? Why? What did you learn from that kid's experience?
- Did anyone pick on other kids? What happened? Has he ever picked on you?
- Did anything make your intuition go "uh-oh"?
- What's the most interesting thing you learned today?
- Did you have any epic fails today? How did you handle it? What did you learn?
- If you could change one thing about your day, what would it be?
- What was the highlight of your day and what was the low point?
- What are you looking forward to tomorrow?

I think you can see how being asked these questions will lead your kid to think more deeply about his day and encourage him to look for ways to help others, for example, so he can tell you about it later.

My niece and her kids share "roses and thorns" every night during dinner. The roses are good, fun, or interesting things that happened; the thorns are things that made them feel bad, sad, or mad. I love this practice and plan to start using it with my grandchildren during the Sunday dinners we share each week.

The point is to pay attention to and connect with your kid. Commit to giving him at least 15 uninterrupted minutes of your time. Admit it, you spent more time than that standing next to the coffeemaker today listening to your crazy coworker rant about her ex!

Zen and the Art of Conversation With a Kid
Speaking of paying attention, when you do the daily sharing with your tween or teen, you have to actually *listen* to her. She'll know if you're secretly ticking off the seconds until you can get back to your Instagram feed and it'll make her feel like shit. So *be present* with her.

If your brain isn't engaged because you forgot to change that oh-so-important meeting from 10 to 11 tomorrow, call your assistant and let her know so you don't have to worry about it. Then give your undivided attention to your kid.

And don't just listen to her, *hear* her. Acknowledge her feelings, ask probing questions, commiserate, laugh, help her problem-solve. You'll learn things that delight you and you'll learn things that scare the bejesus out of you and require you to look deeper.

The point isn't just to praise the positive and resolve the negative; the point is to share her life, day by day. You won't solve all the problems of the world in 15 minutes, but you'll send the message to your kid that you care about her and are on her side.

Be with your kid on her journey through childhood by sharing this precious time with her. One day you'll look back and wish you had that time with her again. Don't miss a moment of it!

Validation Works
When your kid is sharing, you don't want to just sit there and go "uh-huh, uh-huh." Nor do you want to jump in and tell him what he should do to stop the school bully from singling him out. Below are four simple ways

221

to respond to him that will show him you're paying attention and are on the same page:

Mirroring: This is a way to validate what your kid is saying by reflecting (not parroting, which is irritating) his words back to him. For example, if he says: "Jorge called me a name and I really hate him!" You might ask: "It sounds like Jorge hurt your feelings and that made you feel mad?"

The question mark at the end of your sentence leads your child to go deeper into his feelings. (Note that I didn't tell you to jump in and tell him that he shouldn't say "hate." This isn't the time to be judgmental; it's the time to draw your kid's feelings out so he can explore and work through them.)

When you reflect your son's emotions back to him, it invites him to continue: "Yeah! I'm *really* mad at Jorge! I wish he wouldn't call me names." This then gives you the opportunity to help him problem-solve: "What could you do to let Jorge know that you don't like it when he teases you?"

Now the ball is in your kid's court. Zip your piehole and let him think about it; I guarantee he'll come up with a workable solution on his own.

If he throws out a zinger: "I could punch him in his stupid face!" gently guide him to think about more constructive options: "OR... what about talking to him? What could you say?" The point is, don't TELL him what to do; help him think it through until he has a solid plan. (Be sure to teach your kid the ideas I share in Chapter 6 on how to train bullies to leave him alone.)

Clarifying: Asking clarifying questions enables you to draw your kid out and dig deeper into a story or issue. Some examples include: "Can you tell me more about that?" and "I'm not sure I understand. Do you mean...?"

Paraphrasing: Paraphrasing is similar to mirroring, but rather than seeking to validate, you're looking for clarification: "It sounds like you're saying you wish Jorge wouldn't pick on you. Have I got that right?" This is really helpful for kids because it helps them identify big emotions they may not know how to express.

Summarizing: When your kid has reached a conclusion in a story he's telling or a problem he's figured out, you can help him by summarizing what he's said or decided: "So tomorrow you're going to talk to Jorge to let him know that it hurts your feelings when he calls you names and that you'd like him to stop. Have I got that right?" Asking this last question gives him the chance to correct you if you heard him incorrectly or to add more to it.

If He Discloses Something

When you ask the question, "Did anyone pick on other kids? What happened? Has he ever picked on you?" your child may drop a truth bomb in the middle of the conversation, telling you that he's being bullied in a more serious way. Your first reaction may be to rush in and fix everything for him.

Not so fast. Hear him out, try to get to the bottom of the situation to see how serious it is, and determine whether you need to step in (if it's gotten physical, DO step in) or if your child can work this out himself.

Kids disagree, they fight, they call each other names... and then they often resolve it quickly all by their little selves. Your job isn't to go into lecture mode and tell him how to fix things; it's to help him figure things out for himself by asking what *he* thinks he should do.

But if, when you ask the question, "Did anything make your intuition go 'uh-oh'?" your child says yes and discloses any type of abuse, stay calm and ask for more information. Then, after you're done talking to him, handle that shit *tout suite*. Immediately report what you learned to the school, police, and/or Child Protective Services.[xxxiii]

---

xxxiii For more on how to handle a situation like this, see the article on my website at www.cjscarlet.com/freebies entitled "If Your Child Has Been Sexually Abused."

Taking Advantage of Teachable Moments

Outside of your daily check-ins, you'll have plenty of spontaneous conversations that can be turned into body safety teachable moments. This may be while you're riding in the car together or eating ice cream at the mall.

You could play the "what if"[194] game, asking questions like:

- What would you do if someone made you feel really uncomfortable or tried to hurt or touch you in a way you didn't like?
- What if this person was someone you knew?
- What if this person asked you to keep a secret?

These questions and others that I've mentioned earlier in this book offer your kid the chance to talk through how he'd respond to tricky situations. Don't just jump into the yucky scenarios right off the bat, rather, start with more innocuous questions like: "What's the first thing you would do if I told you that you could go over to Dana's house to play video games?" (Correct answer: "I'd call you as soon as I got to her house to tell you I made it safely.")

Your response: "Good! That's right! And what if, on the way to Dana's, another kid asked you to come play with them first?" Correct answer: "I'd tell them I have to ask you for permission first. So, I'd go right to Dana's and call you to ask for permission."

See how one "what if" question leads naturally to the next? You and your kid will quickly get the gist of the game and have fun playing it.

Monthly Family Meetings

Daily check-ins are great and they're an important way to stay in close touch with your individual child's feelings and experiences on a day-to-day basis. Family meetings, on the other hand, are for talking through big issues that affect your whole family, like discussing family values or body safety topics, choosing where to go for an upcoming vacation, or announcing a major transition like a move to a new city.

Family meetings serve a number of purposes, including:

- **Reducing stress:** You can get everyone on the same page by syncing calendars and expectations.

- **Bringing dads into the loop:** Let's get real here; moms do the lioness' share of the work when it comes to managing the household and caring for the kids. (No offense meant, dads, but seriously, you've GOT to step it up! Props to the dads who are carrying their weight and to single dads who are carrying it all!) Family meetings give slacker dads a chance to bond, clue them into what's going on with the rest of the fam, and make them part of the team.

- **Building a strong foundation:** Families that communicate regularly and have each other's backs are families that can weather any storm together.

- **Clearing the air:** When families create time to discuss issues affecting their members, problems don't fester and turn into crises.

- **Teaching your kid valuable life skills:** During family meetings, your kid will learn about cooperation and compromise, leadership, and decision-making, all of which will increase her social skills and self-esteem.

Introducing the Idea

Your tween or teen might complain about the idea of introducing regular family meetings, but if you tell her they'll be followed by food and fun, she'll be more open to the idea. Associating family meetings with pizza and games will make everyone look forward to them and want to participate.

Make it clear to your kid that while you, as the parent(s) have the final say in all matters, her input is encouraged and will be respected. Whenever possible, let her make the decisions that will impact her.

Family Meeting Guidelines

Family meetings will work best if you have clear guidelines everyone can follow. Here are some guidelines to consider:

- **Create a schedule and block it off on your calendar.** I recommend choosing a day and time each month that's easy to remember, say, the first or last Sunday of the month at 5 p.m. (if you plan on having a pizza party and games afterward) or after your usual family dinner. Weekends are best because there's less competition from work or school projects and, thus, less stress.

- **Rotate meeting responsibilities.** Have family members take turns being the leader, secretary, and timekeeper. Playing these roles will teach your kid leadership skills and responsibility and make her feel important.

- **The leader follows the agenda.** The secretary takes notes on the topics that are discussed, decisions that are made, and issues that are placed in the "parking lot" (meaning they're to be discussed later in the meeting or at the next meeting). The timekeeper makes sure the meeting moves along at a brisk pace and doesn't go off on a tangent. The length of the meeting will vary according to what you cover but shoot for 20-30 minutes.

- **Discuss one topic and solve just one problem at a time.** If the conversation gets off base with too many issues being batted around, the leader should pull in the reins, remind everyone what the topic on the table is, and ask the secretary to put all other issues in the "parking lot" list to revisit later.

- **Only one person talks at a time.** Teach your kid how to respectfully listen to others by ensuring only one person speaks at a time. Consider using a "talking stick." This could be as simple as a stick from the backyard, but it would be more fun and special if you and your kid choose something meaningful, like a cool bedazzled wand or something that you decorate together. Choose an object your kid will respect as denoting the holder's right to speak their truth.

- **Create a "no judgment" zone.** At the beginning of each meeting, remind your family members that no thought, emotion, or idea is off the table (within the bounds of good behavior and decency, of course). Especially when it comes to the Q&A portion of the body safety lessons, you don't want to stifle or shame your child.

- Use "I" messages. Saying: "When you do X, I feel angry" is more productive than if you say in a blaming voice: "You make me angry." (After all, no one can make us *feel* anything. We always have a choice in how we respond. Yes, we do. Don't argue with me on this because I'll prove you wrong!)
- Celebrate each other. People, especially kids, are positively starving for validation and recognition. Many of us never got that from our families when we were growing up. Don't be that parent. Lavishly celebrate one another's accomplishments.

What to Cover in Your Family Meetings

It's really important to establish a routine with your family meetings so they're both fun and productive. Consider including the following:

- The designated leader opens with a favorite quote, story, or prayer.
- The leader goes over the agenda, so that everyone knows what to expect.
- The secretary reads the ground rules:
  - This is a safe, confidential space. No one will share what we talk about outside the family unless given permission to do so.
  - Speak your truth, using "I" statements.
  - Everyone is to be respectful and treated with respect in return.
  - Only one person talks at a time. Everyone else listens.
  - It's okay to disagree but keep it kind. No yelling or finger-pointing allowed.
- A parent talks about the body safety topic of the month.[xxxiv]
- Q&A on the body safety topic.

[xxxiv] Choose from among the many body safety topics I cover in this book. For example, you may talk about how to deal with bullies one month and then talk about practicing safe screen time the next. To make it easier, just follow Parts II, III, and IV in order.

- Role-playing on the body safety topic. Make your kid repeat what you've taught her and make her show you, rather than tell you, how she'd react to a threatening situation or person.
- Make decisions as a family about things like vacations and family activities. To reach a decision, do the following:
  - Lay out the idea for everyone to consider.
  - Let each person take a turn sharing their perspective and suggestions. Use the talking stick to keep the conversation under control.
  - Discuss the pros and cons of each suggestion on the table.
  - Make a decision or agree on a solution. Remember that you (and your partner) have the final say, but you want to let your kid's suggestions count. (If you overrule her choice, let her down easy, saying: "You have really great ideas. I don't think we're ready yet as a family for another dog, but we can discuss it again in six months," or something like that.) Choose her ideas whenever you can.
  - Develop a plan of action, including who's responsible for each task and when they need to do them. Make sure you give your kid at least one task that's her responsibility.
- Share information that will affect all family members (e.g., a change in your child's school schedule or routine, an upcoming move, etc.).
- Plan and coordinate weekly schedules.
- Always end with a "freaking lovefest!" When I was the CEO of an international coaching company, my team always ended every business retreat with a freaking lovefest. It's simple: You pick one person at a time to be the object of everyone's attention. One by one, each family member tells the person who's "on the spot" something they really love about them.
- Once everyone else has shared something with that person, you move on to the next person who becomes the center of attention. Get creative and specific. Don't lame out and say: "I love you because you're kind." Say instead: "I love the way you share with your little brother. That's so kind of you. You're a great big sister."
- Bring it in for a hug!

Badass Grandma's Two Cents

Regular family meetings are fun and productive, but it's even more important to do the daily check-ins with your kid. It keeps your finger on the pulse of your child's physical well-being and emotional state and ensures you can quickly respond to anything concerning.

Kids crave attention and affection, especially from their parents (yes, even if they deny it). Your time and undivided attention are like the sunlight, water, and nutrients they need to grow into stable, healthy adults.

Provide these and watch your kid blossom!

Helping You Bring It All Together

Raising Badass Kids 21-Day Action Plan
www.cjscarlet.com/21DayActionPlan

One of the biggest obstacles most parents face after reading my books is how to implement the advice I share—they simply don't know where or how to begin the body safety conversation with their kids and keep it going.

So instead of moving forward, they put off these critical conversations, banking on the hope that their kids won't be exposed to any of the dangers I address.

But burying your head in the sand will leave your kids defenseless and make them even *more* vulnerable to predators.

That's why I want to provide you with a clear action plan on what to do next.

Here's the plan:
Twice a week, over the next 21 days, I'm going to send you an email to walk you through some simple steps to get the conversation rolling with your kids.

It's super simple. We'll start by dividing the 21-day timeframe into three 1 week phases:

1. **Week 1: Getting the Lay of the Land**
Over the next week, we'll begin by helping your child identify who they can trust and, most importantly, how to tell if someone isn't trustworthy.

Through two super simple exercises, you'll be able to unearth any past or existing issues that you'll need to address.

You'll work on:

a. Completing the "Safe People" exercise

b. Completing the "Trust Circle" exercise

c. Taking action (if you learn they're being bullied/abused)

2. Week 2: Entering Your Child's World through Daily Check-Ins

In this next week, we'll introduce daily check-ins with your kid to ensure you're in the loop and on top of the fun, scary, embarrassing, and exciting events of their life.

You'll also help them set strong physical and emotional boundaries, while establishing yourself as a safe person your kid can come to with questions and concerns.

You'll work on:

a. Completing the Strong Boundaries worksheet

b. Giving your kid a "get out of jail free" card

c. Starting daily check-ins

3. Week 3: Bringing it all together

In the last week, you'll plan and hold your first monthly family meeting, where you'll work to get your family on the same page and introduce the first body safety topic.

You'll also continue your daily check-ins with your child, making it a habit that lasts throughout their time in your home.

You'll use the:

a. Monthly family meetings guidelines

b. First body safety topic worksheet

Following this 21-day plan and doing the exercises will allow you to establish a closer relationship with your child, leading to engaging, two-way conversations that show them you're paying attention and have their back.

It will also enable you to spot problems, clear up misunderstandings, and open up opportunities to talk at a deeper level about any issues that are on your kid's mind—*making YOU a seriously Badass Parent!*

Sign up NOW for this free 30-day Action Plan and
start being the parent your child deserves!
Here's the link: *www.cjscarlet.com/21DayActionPlan*

Badass Grandma's Final Thoughts

NO!

I wish I had the power to teach that word to every child in the world and give them permission to use it when they feel uncomfortable or threatened. It sure would have saved me a lot of pain and trauma. It can save your kid too.

I've been a professional writer for more than 40 years now and I can honestly say that writing my *Badass Parenting* books has been the most grueling, heart-wrenching, mind-numbing, and gratifying work I've ever done. It's been a genuine labor of love, one I undertook initially to protect my own sweet grandbabies, but which grew into a larger mission to protect every child on the planet.

My goal is to shift the current paradigm in which kids are pretty much left to figure things out for themselves to one in which parents empower their kids to be safe, savvy, and confident.

I believe with all my heart that if every parent would apply what I teach in this guide, we could dramatically and perhaps even permanently alter the cycle of violence against children that has plagued our society for as long as humans have walked the earth.

What You (Hopefully) Learned

In *Raising Badass Kids,* I taught you how to help your tween or teen learn to set and maintain strong boundaries, trust her gut, and take action to enforce those boundaries and act on her intuition. In the process, you learned a TON of new facts, stats, and probably more information than you bargained for about the dangers and dangerous people your kid might encounter.

If some chapters made you wince or had your head spinning, I apologize. These are not pretty subjects we covered, but I hope the occasional spot of humor helped the medicine go down a bit easier.

My job as the Badass Grandma is to make *your* job as a parent easier and less stressful. Hopefully, you found everything you need in this guide. If you were left with unanswered questions, I'd be happy to answer them for you if I can. Just ping me on the contact page of my website at www. cjscarlet.com/contact or email me directly at cj@cjscarlet.com. I'll also post your questions on the website to ensure everyone has access to my answers.

Finally, if you have kids in the zero to nine age range, I *highly* encourage you to read one of my first books in this series: *Badass Parenting* or *Heroic Parenting*. Both books have the same content, but *Heroic Parenting* is PG-rated while *Badass Parenting* most definitely is NOT.

Thank you, from the bottom of my heart, for sticking with me and for being the parent your kid deserves.

You, my dear, are a seriously badass parent!

P.S. *Did I ever tell you that you're my favorite? :-)*

❧

About the Author

CJ Scarlet, aka the "Badass Grandma," is a danger expert, victim advocate, and crime survivor herself. She's also the doting grandma to three precocious youngsters. CJ has helped thousands of crime victims, but when confronted with the simple innocence of her grandchildren, she felt utterly helpless. How to protect them? More importantly, how to teach them to protect themselves?

Raising Badass Kids: The Savvy Parents' Guide to Predator Proofing Tweens & Teens is CJ's way of doing just that and, in the process, helping parents protect their loved ones too.

An expert in victims' rights and advocacy, CJ has given speeches and workshops at national and international events and has appeared on numerous radio and television programs, including *MSNBC, PBS*, and *NPR*.

The former roller-skating carhop, forest firefighter, and U.S. Marine photojournalist holds an interdisciplinary master's degree in humanities with an emphasis on human violence from Old Dominion University.

Named one of the "Happy 100" people on the planet, CJ's story of triumph over adversity is featured in two bestselling books, including *Happy for No Reason* and *Be Invincible*.

Also by CJ Scarlet

- *The Badass Girl's Guide: Uncommon Strategies to Outwit Predators*
- *Badass Parenting: An Irreverent Guide to Raising Safe, Savvy, Confident Kids*
- *Heroic Parenting: An Essential Guide to Raising Safe, Savvy, Confident Kids*
- *Neptune's Gift: Discovering Your Inner Ocean*

≈

If you enjoyed this book, please post a review on Amazon to encourage others to read it so they can protect their kids too. *(I really appreciate it!)*

Sign up for CJ Scarlet's FREE parenting resources and blog at www.cjscarlet.com.

To reach CJ Scarlet for media inquiries and parent coaching, or to talk to her about her books, contact her at cj@cjscarlet.com.

Bark Discount Code

When you use my affiliate link, you'll receive a discount on Bark's app, phone, or in-hone filtering products. Head to http://bit.ly/CJScarlet, or use the QR code below.

Bark has your back and so do I!

Acknowledgments

I simply could not have conceived of or written this life-changing book without the support, encouragement, and love of the following people:

- To my amazing peeps with Project Vesuvius—Milada Kurucova, Phil Imperial, and Kevin Spencer—for helping me keep it real and on point.
- To the wonderful people at Turkeyland Cove Foundation for gifting me with another magical retreat at the Treehouse so I could write the first draft of this book. Thank you, Kitty Burke and Barbara Welsh for making me feel so welcome and my stay so productive!
- To my publisher, Karen Strauss, and her entire team for helping polish this book until it shined.
- And finally, to you, dear reader, for fighting the good fight every single day to keep your kids safe. May you and they rest easy, knowing you are loved and protected always.

Peace.

The Badass Grandma

End Notes

1. Hillis S, Mercy J, Amobi A, and Kress H. Global prevalence of past-year violence against children: a systematic review and minimum estimates. Pediatrics 2016;137(3): e2015407.
2. Plunkett et al, 2001, from *Body Safety Education* by Jayneen Sanders.
3. Polaris Analysis of2021 Data from theNational HumanTrafficking Hotline.https://polarisproject.org/wp-content/uploads/2020/07/Polaris-Analysis-of-2021-Data-from-the-National-Human-Trafficking-Hotline.pdf
4. Finkelhor, D. (2012). Characteristics of crimes against juveniles, Crimes against Children Research Center.
5. Federal Bureau of Investigation, www.fbi.gov.
6. National Center for Missing and Exploited Children, https://www.missingkids.org/footer/media/keyfacts.
7. https://safeatlast.co/blog/child-abduction-statistics/#gref
8. Federal Bureau of Investigation, www.fbi.gov
9. https://www.fbi.gov/file-repository/2022-ncic-missing-person-and-unidentified-person-statistics.pdf/view
10. Federal Bureau of Investigation, www.fbi.gov
11. https://reason.com/2017/03/31/kidnapping-stats/
12. http://www.pollyklaas.org/about/national-child-kidnapping.html
13. Finkelhor, D., & Jones, L. (2012). Have sexual abuse and physical abuse declined since the 1990s? Crimes against Children Research Center. http://www.unh.edu/ccrc/pdf/CV267_Have%20SA%20%20PA%20Decline_FACT%20SHEET_11-7-12.pdf.

14. Pinker, Steven, *The Better Angels of Our Nature: Why Violence Has Declined*.

15. Pew Research Center.

16. Pinker, Steven, *The Better Angels of Our Nature: Why Violence Has Declined*.

17. http://www.dallasnews.com/opinion/sunday-commentary/20100326-Joe-Keohane-The-crime-wave-762.ece

18. Goeway, Don Joseph,The End of Stress: Four Steps to Rewire Your Brain (New York: Atria, 2014).

19. According to the Census Bureau's 2005 American Community Survey.

20. Bagley, 1995.

21. Dr. William C. Holmes, 1998 study published in the *Journal of the American Medical Association*.

22. National Institute of Mental Health research by Dr. Gene Abel, 1985.

23. www.ChildLuresPrevention.com

24. I Ibid.

25. Finkelhor, David; Ormrod, Richard; and Chaffin, Mark. Juveniles Who Commit Sex Offenses Against Minors. Juvenile Justice Bulletin, December 2009.

26. Rennison, Callie Marie, Ph.D., Intimate Partner Violence and Age of Victim, 1993-99. http://bjs.ojp.usdoj.gov/content/pub/pdf/ipva99.pdf.

27. U.S. Department of Justice, Office of Juvenile Justice and Delinquency Prevention.

28. Center for Sex Offender Management, 1999.

29. Finkelhor, David, and Gewirtz-Meydan, Ateret, 2018. https://theconversation.com/sexual-assault-among-adolescents-6-facts-103658.

30. Flanagan and Hayman-White, 1999.

31. Ibid.

32. Finkelhor, David, and Gewirtz-Meydan, Ateret, 2018. https://theconversation.com/sexual-assault-among-adolescents-6-facts-103658.

33. https://www.verywellmind.com/facts-about-sibling-sexual-abuse-2610456

34. "Women's Health," June/July 2004, Family Violence Prevention Fund and Advocates for Youth, http://www.med.umich.edu/whp/newsletters/summer04/p03-dating.html.

35. Fifth & Pacific Companies, Inc. (Liz Claiborne, Inc.), Conducted by Teen Research Unlimited, (May 2009). "TroubledEconomy Linked to High Levels of Teen Dating Violence & Abuse Survey 2009," https://www.breakthecycle.org/surveys.

36. Department of Justice, Bureau of Justice and Statistics, Intimate Partner Violence in the United States, 1993-2004. Dec. 2006.

37. Jay G. Silverman, PhD; Anita Raj, PhD; Lorelei A. Mucci, MPH; Jeanne E. Hathaway, MD, MPH, "Dating Violence Against Adolescent Girls and Associated Substance Use, Unhealthy Weight Control, Sexual Risk Behavior, Pregnancy, and Suicidality" JAMA. 2001;286(5):572-579. doi:10.1001/jama.286.5.572.

38. Decker M, Silverman J, Raj A. 2005. Dating Violence and Sexually Transmitted Disease/HIV Testing and Diagnosis Among Adolescent Females. Pediatrics. 116: 272-276.

39. D. M. Ackard, Minneapolis, MN, and D. Neumark-Sztainer, Division of Epidemiology, School of Public Health, University of Minnesota, Minneapolis, MN, Date Violence and Date Rape Among Adolescents: Associations with Disordered Eating Behaviors and Psychological Health, Child Abuse & Neglect, 26 455-473, (2002).

40. Emily Rothman and Megan Bair-Merritt, Love or Abuse? Many Teens Can't Tell the Difference, November 23, 2016.

41. Rhode Island Rape Crisis Center Surveys, 1988 and 1998.

42. Sedlak AJ, Mettenburg J, Basena M, et al. Fourth National Incidence Study of Child Abuse and Neglect, Report to Congress. 2010.

43. Kovacs, Steve, Protect Your Kids! The Simple Keys to Children's Safety and Survival.

44. According to a 2000 report commissioned by the American Association of University Women.

45. America After 3PM, Afterschool Alliance and JC Penney Afterschool.

46. Educator Sexual Abuse, Charol Shakeshaft. Department of Foundations, Leadership and Policy Studies.

47. Ibid.

48. Stafford A, et al. Childhood.2015;22:121-137, http://bit.ly/2EifUly.

49. Mountjoy M, et al. Br J Sports Med. 2016;50:1019-1029, http://bjsm.bmj.com/content/50/17/1019.

50. Truth Project Thematic Report: Child sexual abuse in the context of religious institutions, May 2019.

51. Adolescents at Work: Gender Issues and Sexual Harassment, Susan Fineran, August 1, 2002.

52. Ibid.

53. Center for Disease Control, National Center for Injury Prevention and Control (2012). Understanding bullying. http://www.cdc.gov/violenceprevention/pdf/bullyingfactsheet2012-a.pdf.

54. Ibid.

55. Ibid.

56. Carpenter, Deborah, The Everything Parent's Guide to Dealing with Bullies: From playground teasing to cyberbullying, all you need to ensure your child's safety and happiness.

57. Ibid.

58. Ahmed, Sara. Why Aren't We Talking About This Dangerous Type of Bullying? https://www.popsugar.com/family/What-Relational-Bullying-43728079.

59. Carpenter, Deborah, The Everything Parent's Guide to Dealing with Bullies: From playground teasing to cyberbullying, all you need to ensure your child's safety and happiness.

60. Ibid.

61. Miller, Susan, *Gen Z is driving force among adults identifying as LGBTQ, poll shows. Here's a breakdown.* USA Today, Feb. 22, 2023, https://www.usatoday.com/story/news/nation/2023/02/22/gallup-poll-lgbtq-identification/11309075002/.

62. Newport, Frank, Politics, May 22, 2018.

63. From the 2013 National School Climate Survey.

64. Koplewicz, Harold S., M.D. LGBT Teens, Bullying, and Suicide: What are the causes and how can we help?

65. Carpenter, Deborah, The Everything Parent's Guide to Dealing with Bullies: From playground teasing to cyberbullying, all you need to ensure your child's safety and happiness.

66. Gini, G., and Espelage, D. D. (2014) Peer victimization, cyberbullying, and suicide risk in children and adolescents, JAMA Pediatrics, http://jamanetwork.com/journals/jama/article-abstract/1892227.

67. De Becker, Gavin. Protecting the Gift.

68. Weinberger, Jesse. *The Boogeyman Exists, And He's In Your Child's Back Pocket: Internet Safety Tips For Keeping Your Children Safe Online, Smartphone Safety, Social Media Safety, and Gaming Safety.*

69. Petrosina, Guckenburg, Devoe, and Hanson, 2010.

70. Jennifer Hancock, The Bully Vaccine: How to Inoculate Yourself Against Bullies and Other Petty People.

71. Ibid.

72. Ibid.

73. Nixon, C. (2014). Current perspectives: The impact of cyberbullying on adolescent health. Adolescent Health, Medicine and Therapeutics, 5

74. Pew Internet and American Life Project.

75. Carpenter, Deborah, The Everything Parent's Guide to Dealing with Bullies: From playground teasing to cyberbullying, all you need to ensure your child's safety and happiness.

76. Weinberger, Jesse. The Boogeyman Exists; And He's In Your Child's Back Pocket: Internet Safety Tips For Keeping Your Children Safe Online, Smartphone Safety, Social Media Safety, and Gaming Safety

77. Weinberger, Jesse, The Boogeyman Exists; And He's In Your Child's Back Pocket: Internet Safety Tips For Keeping Your Children Safe Online, Smartphone Safety, Social Media Safety, and Gaming Safety.

78. 2013, Ditch the Label: Cyberbullying Statistics.

79. Pew Internet Research Center, FOSI, Cable in the Classroom, 2011.

80. Weinberger, Jesse, The Boogeyman Exists; And He's In Your Child's Back Pocket: Internet Safety Tips For Keeping Your Children Safe Online, Smartphone Safety, Social Media Safety, and Gaming Safety.

81. Munchausen's Syndrome involves a person faking an illness or injury to get attention.

82. Englander, Elizabeth, PhD, Digital Self Harm: Frequency, Type, Motivations, and Outcomes.

83. Carpenter, Deborah, The Everything Parent's Guide to Dealing with Bullies: From playground teasing to cyberbullying, all you need to ensure your child's safety and happiness.

84. https://www.usatoday.com/story/news/nation/2020/10/22/coronavirus-child-abuse-nj-online-child-exploitation-reports-increase/6004205002/

85. https://www.missingkids.org/blog/2021/rise-in-online-enticement-and-other-trends--ncmec-releases-2020-

86. Weinberger, Jesse. The Boogeyman Exists; And He's In Your Child's Back Pocket: Internet Safety Tips For Keeping Your Children Safe Online, Smartphone Safety, Social Media Safety, and Gaming Safety.

87. Ibid

88. GuardChild, The National Campaign to Prevent Teen Pregnancy. "Teenage Sexting Statistics."

89. Weinberger, Jesse. The Boogeyman Exists; And He's In Your Child's Back Pocket: Internet Safety Tips For Keeping Your Children Safe

Online, Smartphone Safety, Social Media Safety, and Gaming Safety.

90. https://pediatrics.aappublications.org/content/143/5/e20183183. abstract

91. Ibid

92. Ibid

93. Ibid

94. Ibid

95. Ibid

96. www.computer.howstuffworks.com

97. Weinberger, Jesse, The Boogeyman Exists and He's In Your Child's Back Pocket: Internet Safety Tips For Keeping Your Children Safe Online, Smartphone Safety, Social Media Safety, and Gaming Safety.

98. Ibid.

99. Ibid

100. Cox, Brian. Child Safety & Protection: Child Security for Parents & Children (A Safety Crusaders Project Book 1).

101. New research finds 95% of teens have access to a smartphone; 45% online 'almost constantly' by Kurt Schlosser on June 1, 2018

102. https://www.tandfonline.com/doi/abs/10.1080/10810730.2021.188 7980

103. https://www.bitdefender.com/news/bitdefender-study-shows-95-of-parents-found-children-accessing-internet-pornography-1999.html

104. https://www.justia.com/criminal/offenses/sex-crimes/child-pornography/

105. https://www.psychologytoday.com/us/blog/real-healing/201208/ overexposed-and-under-prepared-the-effects-early-exposure-sexual-content

106. www.GuardChild.com

107. https://perfectionpending.net/kids-and-pornography-the-statistics-every-parent-needs-to-know-and-how-you-can-protect-your-kids-online/

108. Wolak, Janis, J.D.; Finkelhor, David, Ph.D.; Walsh, Wendy, Ph.d.; and Treitman, Leah. Crimes against Children Research Center, University of New Hampshire, www.wearethorn.org.

109. https://parentology.com/how-to-talk-to-your-teen-about-sexting/?utm_source=newsletter&utm_medium=email&utm_campaign=recess_reading_08_25_2019

110. Kristen A. Jenson, MA, *The Shocking Tactics Sex Traffickers Use to Trap Your Kids and 5 Ways You Can Protect Them*, Oct. 13, 2020. https://www.defendyoungminds.com/post/shocking-tactics-sex-traffickers-use-trap-your-kids-5-ways-you-can-protect-them?ck_subscriber_id=548470620&utm_source=convertkit&utm_medium=email&utm_campaign=%E2%9A%A1The+Most+Dangerous+Myth+about+Child+Sex+Trafficking+and+3+Ways+to+Keep+Your+Kid+Safe%20-%207356207.

111. https://www.missingkids.org/gethelpnow/cybertipline

112. "Sex and tech". The National Campaign to Prevent Teen and Unplanned Pregnancy, December 10, 2008.

113. Best Apps & Devices To Monitor Your Kids Online Activity, By Zahra, last updated Jul 17, 2019.

114. https://www.stopitnow.org/ohc-content/defining-child-sexual-abuse

115. Finkelhor, David, Characteristics of crimes against juveniles. Crimes against Children Research Center, 2012.

116. https://www.d2l.org/wp-content/uploads/2017/01/all_statistics_20150619.pdf

117. Ibid.

118. Sedlak, et al. (2010). Fourth National Incidence Study of Child Abuse and Neglect: Report to Congress, U.S. Department of Health and Human Services, Administration for Children and Families.

119. Ibid.

120. Finkelhor, David, Current information on the scope and nature of child sexual abuse. The Future of Children, Vol. 4, No. 2, Sexual Abuse of Children, 1994.

121. Ibid.

122. Sedlak, et al. (2010). Fourth National Incidence Study of Child Abuse and Neglect: Report to Congress, U.S. Department of Health and Human Services, Administration for Children and Families.

123. Ibid.

124. Finkelhor, D.; Ormrod, R.K.; and Turner, H.A. (2010). Poly-victimization in a national sample of children & youth. American Journal of Preventive Medicine.

125. Ibid.

126. Ibid.

127. Putnam, F. (2003). Ten-year research update review: child sexual abuse. Journal of American Child Adolescence Psychiatry, 42(3).

128. Krebs, Christopher P.; Lindquist, Christine H.; Warner, Tara D.; Fisher, Bonnie S.; Martin, Sandra L. (2009). "College Women's Experiences with Physically Forced, Alcohol- or Other Drug-Enabled, and Drug-Facilitated Sexual Assault Before and Since Entering College". Journal of American College Health.

129. https://www.d2l.org/wp-content/uploads/2017/01/all_statistics_20150619.pdf

130. Ibid.

131. Boyer, Deborah and Fine, David. Sexual Abuse as a Factor in Adolescent Pregnancy and Child Maltreatment. Family Planning Perspectives, Vol. 24, No. 1 (Jan/Feb 1992).

132. Duke University. Dropping out of high school linked to child abuse. ScienceDaily. ScienceDaily, December 1, 2017. www.sciencedaily.com/releases/2017/12/171201131636.htm

133. Ibid.

134. Ibid.

135. Sachs-Ericsson, N., Blazer, D., Plant, E. A., & Arnow, B. (2005). Childhood sexual and physical abuse and 1-year prevalence of medical problems in the National Comorbidity Survey. Health Psychology, 24.

136. https://www.rainn.org/articles/talking-your-kids-about-sexual-assault

137. https://www.bustle.com/p/13-sex-trafficking-statistics-that-put-the-worldwide-problem-into-perspective-9930150

138. "The Commercial Sexual Exploitation of Children in the U. S., Canada and Mexico. https://web.archive.org/web/20081002000344/http://www.sp2.upenn.edu/~restes/CSEC_Files/Exec_Sum_020220.pdf.

139. Ibid

140. https://arkofhopeforchildren.org/child-trafficking/child-trafficking-statistics

141. www.PolarisProject.org

142. According to Russ Tuttle of The Stop Trafficking Project, https://www.defendyoungminds.com/post/shocking-tactics-sex-traffickers-use-trap-your-kids-5-ways-you-can-protect-them?ck_subscriber_id=548470620&utm_source=convertkit&utm_medium=email&utm_campaign=%E2%9A%A1The+Most+Dangerous+Myth+about+Child+Sex+Trafficking+and+3+Ways+to+Keep+Your+Kid+Safe%20-%207356207.

143. https://arkofhopeforchildren.org/child-trafficking/child-trafficking-statistics

144. Ibid

145. National Institute of Justice. (2007). Commercial sexual exploitation of children: What do we know and what do we do about it? (Publication NCJ 215733). U.S. Department of Justice. Office of Justice Programs.

146. https://arkofhopeforchildren.org/child-trafficking/child-trafficking-statistics

147. Ibid

148. https://www.collectiveshout.org/what_we_know_about_men_who_buy_sex

149. Dutton; Painter (1981). "Traumatic Bonding: The development of emotional attachments in battered women and other relationships of intermittent abuse". *Victimology: An International Journal* (7).

150. https://www.cnn.com/2016/07/13/opinions/5-disguises-human-trafficker/index.html

151. www.Love146.org

152. National Center for Missing & Exploited Children.

153. http://cybersafewomen.org/how_cyber_criminals_and_predators_select_their_prey

154. Maslow, Abraham, *A Theory of Human Motivation*, 1943.

155. Black MC, Basile KC, Breiding MJ, Smith SG, Walters ML, Merrick MT, Chen J, Stevens MR. The National Intimate Partner and Sexual Violence Survey (NISVS): 2010 Summary Report. Atlanta, GA: National Center for Injury Prevention and Control, Centers for Disease Control and Prevention, 2011.

156. We're Teaching Consent All Wrong, By Sarah D. Sparks — January 08, 2019, https://www.edweek.org/teaching-learning/were-teaching-consent-all-wrong/2019/01

157. Ibid.

158. Adrienne Santos-Longhurst, Healthline, Your Guide to Consent, https://www.healthline.com/health/parenting/consent-at-every-age.

159. https://parents.au.reachout.com/common-concerns/everyday-issues/things-to-try-talking-about-sex/how-to-teach-your-teenager-about-consent

160. https://cougarhealth.wsu.edu/2016/11/09/guide-verbal-non-verbal-consent/, published on Nov. 9, 2016.

161. Adrienne Santos-Longhurst, Healthline, Your Guide to Consent, https://www.healthline.com/health/parenting/consent-at-every-age.

162. Abbey, Antonia, PhD, Alcohol-Related Sexual Assault: A Common Problem among College Students, https://www.ncbi.nlm.nih.gov/pmc/articles/PMC4484270/.

163. Ellsberg, Michael, No-BS Advice For Men About Drugs, Alcohol, and Sexual Consent If you choose to mix alcohol or drugs with sex, be careful..., July 19, 2018, https://goodmenproject.com/featured-content/no-bs-advice-for-men-about-drugs-alcohol-sexual-consent-pgtn/.

164. Weissbourd, Richard, et al, The Talk How Adults Can Promote Young People's Healthy Relationships and Prevent Misogyny and Sexual Harassment, https://static1.squarespace.com/static/5b7c56e255b02c683659fe43/t/5bd51a0324a69425bd079b59/1540692500558/mcc_the_talk_final.pdf.

165. www.NCTSN.org

166. https://www.stopitnow.org/ohc-content/why-sexuality-education-is-an-important-part-of-a-safety-plan

167. https://www.npr.org/2018/01/10/566608390/she-can-t-tell-us-what-s-wrong

168. Ibid.

169. Sorensen, David D. The Invisible Victims, an update of an article originally published in Prosecutor's Brief: the California District Attorneys Associations Quarterly Journal, 2002.

170. Balderian, N. Sexual abuse of people with developmental disabilities, Sexuality and Disability, 1991.

171. Bowman, Rachel A.; Scotti, Joseph R.; Morris, Tracy L. Sexual Abuse Prevention: A Training Program for Developmental Disabilities Service Providers, Journal of Child Sexual Abuse, 2010.

172. Disabilities: Insights from Across Fields and Around the World; Marshall, Kendall, Banks & Gover (Eds.), 2009.

173. British Journal of Learning Support, 2008.

174. U.S. Individuals with Disabilities Education Act.

175. https://www.understood.org/en/school-learning/special-services/
special-education-basics/conditions-covered-under-idea

176. https://studentaffairs.jhu.edu/disabilities/about/types-of-disabilities/

177. https://www.understood.org/en/school-learning/special-services/
special-education-basics/conditions-covered-under-idea

178. https://studentaffairs.jhu.edu/disabilities/about/types-of-disabilities/

179. Ibid.

180. Center for Disease Control and Prevention. (2013). Developmental
disabilities, retrieved October 18, 2013.

181. https://www.t2000.com/what-is-a-developmental-disability/.

182. https://studentaffairs.jhu.edu/disabilities/about/types-of-disabilities/

183. U.S. Department of Education, 2000.

184. Education Law Center, 2002.

185. https://www.equalityhumanrights.com/en/inquiries-and-
investigations/inquiry-disability-related-harassment/background-
disability-related-0

186. https://www.understood.org/en/school-learning/special-services/
special-education-basics/conditions-covered-under-idea

187. https://www.understood.org/en/school-learning/your-childs-rights/
basics-about-childs-rights/individuals-with-disabilities-education-
act-idea-what-you-need-to-know

188. https://www.parentcenterhub.org/iep-overview/

189. www.StopBullying.gov

190. https://www.stopitnow.org/ohc-content/tip-sheet-family-safety-
planning-for-parents-of-children-with-disabilities and https://www.
stopitnow.org/ohc-content/tip-sheet-how-to-talk-to-your-child-to-
reduce-vulnerability-to-sexual-abuse.

191. Conducted by Vera's Center on Victimization and Safety and the Ms.
Foundation for Women.

192. www.vera.org

193. https://www.stopitnow.org/ohc-content/tip-sheet-how-to-protect-your-child-from-sexual-abuse-in-program-setting

194. As described by Gary Martin Hays and Adam Weart in their book, *The Authority on Child Safety: How to Talk to Your Kids About Their Personal Safety Without Scaring Them.*

Printed in the USA
CPSIA information can be obtained
at www.ICGtesting.com
LVHW011240270324
775527LV00013B/594